HERDING OSTRICHES

Six Generations in the Workplace . . .
One Flock of a Problem!

Herding Ostriches

Contributors
Content included by permission of contributors.
John Meluso, johncsp@meluso.com
Seth Johnson, goldenhemloc11@hotmail.com
Kevin Brooks, brucekbrooks@comcast.net

Published by
Blooming Twig Books
320 S. Boston, Suite 1026
Tulsa, OK 74013
Tel: 1-866-389-1482
Fax: 1-866-298-7260
www.bloomingtwig.com

Printed in the United States of America

ISBN 978-1-61343-016-3
First Edition / Galley Print

10 9 8 7 6 5 4 3 2

This book is dedicated to my parents,
Grayson Mallow and Janet Mallow.
Simply put, thank you for everything!

HERDING OSTRICHES

Six Generations in the Workplace . . .
One Flock of a Problem!

Kate Sheridan
GENERATIONAL LEADERSHIP

Blooming Twig Books
New York / Tulsa

Acknowledgments

This book is written with the support and encouragement of many extraordinary people:

My children. Thank you for loving me unconditionally and teaching me patiently.

Steven, Adrienne, Grayson, Sterling, Olivia, and Liam.

My professional colleagues. Thank you for advising me and redirecting me when I lost focus.

Kent Gustavson, PhD., Seth Johnson, M. Ed., John Meluso, CSP, Kevin Brooks, Terry Brock, MA, CSP, CPAE, and Jonathan Peters, PhD.

My friends and family. Thank you for taking time to allow me to vent and helping me to find the humor amidst the chaos.

Scarlet White, Jeff Mallow, Jason Mallow, Tansey Schoonover, Nikki Stevens, Brian Ferris, and Ida Felix.

TABLE OF CONTENTS

HERDING OSTRICHES

Six Generations in the Workplace . . .
One Flock of a Problem!

"You don't direct ostriches,
you herd them."

- Shelly Duvall

INTRODUCTION

"**A**re you pretending to be an ostrich?"

My 8-year-old son asked me that when I was looking for several things at the same time and not finding any of them.

I responded with a smile. "Why would you ask that?"

"Because you're running in circles and look like you have no idea where you are going!"

He waited a moment, then continued, "Do ostriches really think that they are invisible when they put their heads in a hole?"

Though I am familiar with Liam's quick humor, I'm still unsure if he uses it to "mess" with me. I do know that his questions confuse me. I believe that anyone that confuses me is either a complete idiot or a genius. Since he is my son, we're going with genius.

I have a few rules when sparring with a genius. First, look them in the eye. (You don't want them to sense your fear) Second, answer their question with a question to see if they will give you more information. (I used this trick in spelling bees to buy time. "Could you use that word in a sentence?")

When I try to sound intelligent, I end up sounding like Yoda. "Asking a question, are you? Need my insight, do you?" I don't know why it works, it just does.

"I'm not sure if they think that they are invisible. I will have to look that up. How would that be related to me running in circles anyway?"

"Well, I think if they are stupid enough to run in circles when they're confused, they're probably stupid enough to think that no one can see them when their head is in a hole."

Ok, now I know that he's messing with me. It's time for my third rule, mumble something unintelligible, look at my watch and get the heck out of there. Some day Liam is going to notice that I don't wear a watch. Again, I don't know why it works, it just does.

I am pretty sure that I am not a genius. And, as they say, just being able to acknowledge where you are is proof that you are not too far gone.

I teach management seminars for a living. The "kids" in my classes keep looking younger every day. And, they keep getting smarter. I am using my three rules of "genius sparring" more than I'd like to admit.

I do try to keep up. I research their questions in the quiet stillness of my bedroom late at night. Don't take to mean that I am deep. It just means that I can't sleep when I feel stupid.

I looked up my son's. Actually, it's a misnomer. Ostriches do not think that they are invisible with their heads in the ground. (I have no idea who concluded that, or what research was done to know what Ostriches think, but I have to go with Wikipedia on this one.)

Liam was right. Ostriches do run in circles when they are confused. And, since common belief holds that Ostriches think that they are invisible with their heads in a hole, I'm using it. Speakers can get by with that stuff. We have podiums.

I see a direct comparison between an Ostrich's unorthodox methods of handling emotions and those of most company leaders. (This does not include my clients. You guys are brilliant!)

This is not a book on economic projections or international competition. This is a book about a much more manageable and yet much more ignored challenge. There are now five generations of Americans in the workplace. The fifth one spun out on its own within the last year. A sixth one will make its appearance in four short years. Things are about to get wild.

The five principles in Herding Ostriches will keep you from needlessly running in circles. We all want to look like we are in the know, but we can't all have podiums. (Generation Flux just woke up. Hint: Don't tell generation Flux that they can't have what they want.)

In the first principle, we look at the ideology of the four generations that are defined by their birth year. We learn about the Fluxers. They formed their own group within the last few years. They are the only "generation" not defined by a birth year. Finally, we are introduced to the newest generation. They might be working for you in the not-so-distant future.

After we wrap our minds around the chaotic climate created by the generational mixing, we will see how team-building is changing as well. Principle Two will discuss the two types of teams that have always existed. Type 1 has been addressed in countless books and motivational speeches. The second type has largely been ignored. I know. I play for that team. I am miserable if forced to work for Type 1, and I am not alone.

Type 2 is rapidly increasing in numbers. The increase is directly related to the ideology of the latest three generations. Leaders that stick their head in the sand with team-building, will probably see their teams collapse.

The third Principle will be preparing us for the sixth generation. As they are yet to be named, we refer to them here as Gen Next. They were born shortly before and since 911. They have grown up seeing war on television, and hearing financial worries discussed over dinner. They are developing characteristics that align them with the Traditionalists.

Even so, they are going to be undeniably unique. Their traditional values are mixing into a non-traditional world. (They are going to share an enthusiasm for buying clothes at a thrift store with their grandparents, but they are going to clash on the clothes. Hint: tummy-viewing is coming back. Start your sit-ups.)

The fourth principle will help businesses improve their effectiveness when working with a team and/or a customer base that is largely off-site. This trend does not seem to be reversing. Principle four will address call centers, sales teams, and collection companies. When you don't have face-to-face, everything comes down to your word choice.

There is a single word that ignites almost all of our battles. It's tricky. People like us better if we use it wisely. (This one might even improve your sex life) Ok, don't even pretend that you are shocked to see this promise in the Introduction. I don't know why it works, it just does.

The fifth Principle of Herding Ostriches focuses on communication. Relationships are damaged, business deals are destroyed and corporate climates are immobilized when communication sucks. (Yes, I went there.)

Herding Ostriches is written for the progressive company owner, officer, or "career designer". (That's a buzz phrase I invented, feel free to use it.) This book is for leaders that have a passion for staying relevant and competitive. It is designed for the open-minded and adaptable.

The focus of this book is a term we use in our seminars, "generational leadership". We believe that it is the next phase of effective growth for corporations and professionals.

Herding Ostriches also features work of three talented contributors; John Meluso, Seth Johnson, and Kevin Brooks.

We know that you are facing a daunting task in blending six generations into an effective team. We are convinced that this book will help. We want you to know that we believe you can do this. Yes, yes, that phrase is overused. I don't know why it works, it just does.

*"An ostrich with his head in the sand
is just as blind to opportunity as to disaster."*

- Unknown

*"It is not the strongest of the species that survives;
nor the most intelligent that survives.
It is the one that is most adaptable to change."*

- Charles Darwin

Principle One

Generations are changing the Game! This chapter starts out with a general account-taking of your organization, and then proceeds to examine every generation in your workplace. Try to go through this with an open mind!

You will see throughout the chapter that I have interspersed moments where I say "Get your head out of the sand!" and "Stop running in circles!" If you take anything away from reading and working with this book, take those two phrases and concepts!

The most important thing to do when you work through this first principle is to have fun! The more your team knows about one another, the better everything will function, and the more fun it will become for you and all of your colleagues to come to work!

Let's get started!

Get your head out of the sand!

List the characteristics or attributes that you want the leader of your organization to display. The person you want to follow would be:

1._____

2._____

3._____

4._____

5._____

6._____

7._____

8._____

9._____

10._____

Now compare yourself to some of my seminar attendees. Circle any that are also on your list. The list on this page came from a seminar I taught in 2012.

The top 10 attributes I want in my leader:

1.   Great Communicator

2.   Great Listener

3.   Cares about my development

4.   Approachable

5.   Fair

6.   Facilitates Change

7.   Rewards my ideas

8.   Open to growth

9.   Teacher

10.   Honesty

The list on this page came from a seminar I taught in 2004. Can you identify any major differences between the two lists and your list? Again, circle any that are also on your list.

The top 10 attributes I want in my leader:

1. Decisive

2. Risk-Taker

3. Competitive

4. Visionary

5. Able to cast a vision

6. Intelligent

7. Negotiator

8. Knowledgeable

9. Concise

10. Fearless

Were any of your answers on the lists? If so, did you have more in common with the 2012 list or the 2004 list? The 2012 list is largely made up of people skills. The 2004 list is largely hard-edged skills. This undeniable shift is exactly why we are discussing generational leadership.

Being a former journalist (OK, I did sales research for CNN), I can deduce that we are now seeking people skills over hard skills. This is apparent from the boardroom to the White House. This is driven by the generational shift.

The "ah ha" moment comes when we finish the exercise. Which of the hard skills prized 8 years ago would you remove from today's list? How many of the skills of 8 years ago were on your list?

Do I hear silence?

We have been conditioned to connect to certain buzz words and to attach ourselves to qualities that feel good from a leader. In the end, we really want all 20. We are hoping to wrap the harder leadership skills into prettier, more user-friendly paper. Effective leadership is twice as hard to achieve today as it was just eight years ago.

It's important to know how we arrived here.

Herding Ostriches will take a look at all 6 generations and see how each one needs to be managed, led, inspired and incentivized. Specifically, it considers which generation caused which change and helps us to strategize the management of all six at the same time.

At the end of each generational section, there is a system that can be used in "herding" that particular group into a cohesive team.

Stop running in circles!

Daniel Goleman introduced the term "Emotional Intelligence" in 2005. We have had seven years to move to the management techniques that he suggested. Have you?

If not, get his book and have your team read it. Herding Ostriches expands upon his work, taking emotional intelligent leadership and applying it to the generations.

"America cannot be an ostrich
with its head in the sand."

- President Woodrow Wilson

FIVE GENERATIONS

Generations are changing the game! It wasn't until the Baby Boomers arrived to the work force that talk of generations began. Baby boomers caught attention by the magnitude of their numbers. As in any situation where there is over-crowding, an effort ensues to stand out, get competitive, and most importantly, to create new avenues and options.

Baby Boomers are often looked to now as a stuffy, rigid group. That description does not line up with Woodstock, rock-n-roll, recreational drugs, and sit ins. They were rebels and they left their mark. They changed the game.

Baby Boomers brought customer service to the business world. Traditionalists had the manners, but weren't known for reaching beyond that surface level to try to win a customer over. Again, the numbers forced Baby Boomers to look for new ways to beat each other.

After Baby Boomers, Generation X arrived and grabbed the coolest name of them all. Then, they started to change the work force with technology. Bill Gates is from this generation as well as many Fortune 500 leaders that found themselves there in a relatively short time due to innovative start-ups.

Once again, the game changed.

Now, Millennials are everywhere at once. They are pushing hard to get up the ladder, through the skylight, and onto the rooftop to simply sit still and assess their accomplishments with their fellow Millennials.

In four short years, we will get the only generation that might have a chance of taking the reigns from the Millennials, but they will do it with quiet determination and unshakable focus, the Nexters. The game is about to change again.

TRADITIONALISTS (1927–1945)

Traditionalists (aka The Silent Generation) were born between 1927 and 1945. They are in their 60s, 70s and 80s. About 95% of the Traditionalists are retired from the workforce. Those that remain are largely partners, managers, and senior support staff. We do not need to discuss the reasons that some are remaining in the work force, but we can appreciate that they are. This generation has experienced some of the toughest times our country has known in business and they have the clarity and the coping skills necessary to continue to lead in our uncertain business climate.

Traditionalists are hardworking, loyal, submissive, and likely to have stayed with one to three employers in their career. They do not shy away from long hours, unexplained change, showing respect in the face of floundering leadership, nor demonstrating a team mentality even if they don't care too much for the team. Only in the area of technology know-how do they seem to be less than an ideal candidate for most jobs.

In team-building, managers would be wise to respect a team member that has survived decades of change. The challenges for herding these "Ostriches" would be first in the area of encouraging them to speak up, and second in the area of getting them to effectively use all available technology tools.

In meetings, especially meetings that are confrontational, traditionalists are usually content to stay quiet. This comes from a combination of their learned respect of authority and an acceptance of the "chose your battles wisely" philosophy. Simply, they tend to only speak up when called upon. It's time to call on them.

The main responsibility of any Supervisor is to "develop their team". That includes team members that are close to retirement. Though submissive, Traditionalists will rise to the occasion if they are asked to develop new skills.

It troubles me when a company manager tells me that one of their team members is close to retirement so they are going to "let them ride". Really? First, it's not the manager's money. Second, every team member deserves to be developed the entire time that they are with us.

Team leaders that have Traditionalists on their team will benefit from one-on-one conversations. Traditionalists prefer casual, non-confrontational communication. They also prefer that someone else do the presenting at team gatherings. To get the full benefit of their insight, it's a good idea to require every team member to speak up at staff meetings. If everyone presents their two minutes on the floor, Traditionalists will have to participate.

One of the most discouraging things that Traditionalists experience in the workplace is seeing their skills drop through no fault of their own. Technology leaves them behind. At times, it leaves most of us behind. Traditionalists did not grow up with personal computers. That doesn't mean that they are less capable of mastering the latest tools. (They may be the only generation that can program cable and a VCR.) Let's be open to that.

The first thing that needs to happen to integrate them effectively into a team is to respect their talents. They are often very patient and can read people. These are great survival skills.

We will also benefit from their ability to clearly see what should be pursued and what should be released in the economy of the next decade.

It would be smart to assess their knowledge of technology tools. No one benefits from keeping them away from the tools. They need to be patiently developed. It would be wise to put a patient teacher with this student.

One of the most effective training pairings in companies today is putting the youngest team member with the eldest. They blend well.

The success of this odd pairing has to do with the emergence of ideology within Gen Next that is arriving in four years. As generations "blend" into each other, some ideologies overlap.

Though Millennials think differently as a group, the youngest of them are beginning to blend into the ideology of Gen Next. Ideally, the Primaries will soon be training with the Traditionalists. They have much in common.

"Ostrich skeletons and fossils have been found which date back over 120 million years. Ostriches are true dinosaurs!"

- Anonymous

TRADITIONALISTS SUMMARY

- Born between 1927-1945

- They are in their 60's, 70's, and 80's

- 95% are no longer in the work force

- The 5% that remain are largely in customer service or partners, managers and senior support staff

- They are capable of mastering all technology

- They probably need training in technology

- They are loyal

- Unless asked, they rarely offer their opinion

- They relate well to young Millennials and the coming Nexters.

- They understand corporate hierarchy and levels

Get your head out of the sand!

List the names of your team members that you think fall into the Traditionalist generation. Assess their skill level in technology.

Name: Technology Score (1-10)

1._____   _____

2._____   _____

3._____   _____

4._____   _____

5._____   _____

6._____   _____

7._____   _____

8._____   _____

9._____   _____

10._____   _____

Offer training to those that you ranked less than 10!

Again, list the names of the team members that you think fall into the Traditionalist generation. Assess their verbal participation in meetings.

Name: Score Participation 1-10:

1._____   _____

2._____   _____

3._____   _____

4._____   _____

5._____   _____

6._____   _____

7._____   _____

8._____   _____

9._____   _____

10._____   _____

Assign those that ranked less than 10 an active role in your next meeting!

Herding Skill: Manage Your Levels

Traditionalists have been in the work force for decades. Though loyal to employers, many are now with new ones. Even if a traditionalist might have been at the top of a company ladder, changes might find them at the bottom. They often prefer it to be that way. Most are no longer in the competitive mode, but rather in a mode of service and one of seeking an enjoyable work environment.

Over our careers, most of us will shift through at least two of the three levels of the company pyramid. The first level is entry. Sixty-five percent of company employees are in level one. Many people enjoy level one and stay there for their entire careers. Thirty percent are in level two. This level is made up middle management, program directors, and specialists. Five percent are in level three. This is the top of the pyramid and is made up of company owners, CEOS and Industry Experts.

Traditionalists that are managed by others are probably in Level 1. It is important to know where they have been in their career. It is important to tap into their skills and knowledge base. It is also vital to know where they want to go next.

One of the questions I ask supervisors is if they have seen the original resumes or job applications for their team members? Most have not. Most inherited their team. Few hired them.

If you supervise, I suggest that you go to your Human Resource Department and collect that information. Study it. Have it on hand when you conduct career strategy meetings with them.

It will impress any team member, especially a Traditionalist, when they discover that you have studied their career track. You have read their mission statement and career objective.

I suggest that companies have everyone re-write their career objective statement every year as a part of their performance evaluations. They constantly change, especially right now. Performance evaluations should be about employee development, not employee discipline.

The critical part of knowing the career experience of a Traditionalist as well as their goals with your organization is optimizing their contributions. Their contributions are especially valuable at level 1.

Level one has more interaction with customers and peers.

They usually experience less stress. They are more likely to build personal friendships at the office and to continue those friendships off site.

Level one succeeds by having great customer service and conflict resolution skills.

Challenges of managing level one will be in keeping them engaged in and loyal to the company. We must never forget that they are our front line. Customers and clients often stay or leave over their performance. They need career-development meetings as often as other levels.

Level one has a keen sense of what customers need from your company. They often have great ideas of how the company could improve. They are likely to be keeping it to themselves or discussing it with their peers at the water cooler. Wise leaders will cultivate those ideas through constant communication.

Level one also tends to run in cliques. Cliques are dangerous. Cliques usually run in threes. Left alone, they can become bullies and stifle the flow of ideas. At the center of each clique is what I refer to as the clique-master.

I can spot them in meetings. When seated, they are the one sitting in the center of their two clique followers. The followers lean slightly towards the clique-master. The master has excellent communication skills and solid personal power. That is how they gain the loyalty of their peers.

To break up a clique, you will need to shift the loyalty of the two followers from the master to the company and to yourself. Seventy percent of U.S. employees that participate in an exit interview will site their relationship with their immediate supervisor as the reason they are leaving. Less than one-half percent will leave their job because someone else left their's.

In 1993-1999, I managed a mobile-medicine company with a dentist. I had a clique-master. This was my first experience with running my own company and was I was constantly worried about losing team members.

After my time log revealed that my favorite team member had been in my office five times in a given week with conflict with five different co-workers, I realized I had a problem to address.

I asked her to my office and opened the discussion of the conflicts. I will never forget that she was seated in a chair with rolling wheels. As she stared me dead in the eyes, she began edging towards my desk in her moving chair. I started to worry. I began to wonder if she was going to climb over the desk and attack. (I began to wish that I had been taking kick-boxing classes at the gym instead of yoga.)

She put her elbows on my desk and asked if I intended to discipline her? If I did, she assured me that she would quit and that Kim and Karen would leave as well.

I started to run the numbers in my head. Three hygienists gone in a single day each with six-month schedules already set. That might tank us. I backed down. As you may guess, the clique-master intensified. She started to make life miserable for everyone.

Five months later, I released her from her job. She was right. Kim and Karen were in my office within 15 minutes. But, much to my surprise, Kim had come for the clique-master's office and Karen wanted her parking spot. Namaste'!

Turnover is expensive and disruptive. It is important to make every effort to retain every single member of the team. Cliques have to be dissolved. I have found one method to be extremely effective.

Meet with the most-promising of the two followers and offer them an assignment, even temporarily, wherein they directly report to you. Then, do the same with the other one. I assure you that as they leave your office after your private meetings, the clique-master will seek them out to see what is happening. The two will probably say very little about their new assignments. The followers will be turning their loyalty to you and the company. The three will begin to meet up less and stop sitting together in meetings.

Your clique-master will then move in one of three directions. They will seek out new followers (and the process begins again), they will quit, or they will realize that real power comes from compliance and loyalty. Either way they go, your problem is temporarily or permanently handled.

Level 2 is where most new ideas are generated. This happens for two reasons. First, at this level, they have a full 360 degree view of company operations. They have feedback from level three, supervise level one, and have high-level relationships with clients and peers. With clients, they are often conversing with the ones that are either critical to the company or the ones that are dissatisfied and could not get a resolution at level 1. With peers, they are often in strategy sessions or committees were ideas are being shared.

Second, they are more likely to be seen and heard by level 3. They feel empowered to present their ideas. They can visualize that their next big idea could earn them a promotion or buy their way to early retirement. Both are possible.

There are two main challenges to managing level 2. First, is empowering them without having them abuse that power. Second, is having them grow completely into the supervisory role.

The first challenge is going to be the most difficult for a micro-manager to handle. Middle Management expects that their new title comes with autonomy. In most cases, if the right choice was made, they will thrive if left alone. A good due diligence system is one way to see the results of their performance without intruding into their daily operations. Their turnover numbers should to be followed along with production and bottom-line budgets. One way to gage the success of a level 2 is to watch the growth of their team. Level 2s should always be training their replacement. Their team should be growing into new roles and being cross-trained.

The second challenge with level 2 is having them fully embrace leadership. Each level of advancement in leadership comes with more isolation. That isolation is not comfortable for everyone. They have to accept that they might be left out of lunches, company gossip, and water-cooler conversations. The higher the level, the more pronounced the isolation becomes.

Levels 2 and 3 should try to fill that isolation by networking with people outside their company that hold equal positions and face the same challenges. Trying to hang onto relationships with level 1 could sink a level 2.

I was speaking to a group of young supervisors in New York City. One new supervisor wanted to take the floor and share is story of success. His name was Jeremy and he had been promoted to head of shipping and receiving of a big corporation. He told the group that day that the key to his success the four months that he had held the new position was in spending one day a week down in the warehouse packing boxes alongside his guys.

Jeremy told the audience that he did this so that his guys wouldn't think that he thought that he was better than they or that his new title wouldn't make the guys think that he thought that his job was more important than theirs. He received lots of nods from the audience.

As I caught up with him during a break, I asked if we could revisit his comments. As I repeated back to Jeremy what he had said, I put the emphasis on the words he and his. By hearing it back he could see where I was going. He wasn't doing this for his guys, he was doing it for himself. He was afraid to let go and grow into the leadership role that would potentially isolate him. His job was no longer to pack boxes, his job was to ensure that there were boxes to be packed.

I went on to tell Jeremy that if I had been sitting in the audience and was the owner of the company where he was employed, I would have just heard that one of my employees is not doing his job 50 to 52 days a year, and that employee was him.

The part that a new supervisor like Jeremy can often overlook is that if they do not rise up and do their job, there might come a day when they will have to go down to the box-packing area and let one or more guys go because there aren't enough boxes to be packed.

The other thing that they often miss is that though their team might be cordial when they are on site, most of them probably resent it. I told Jeremy that is was likely that there was conversation about him the other four days. His team was likely comparing their box-packing performance to their supervisor and questioning why he was in charge.

Managing level 2 requires handling with kids' gloves. They often want autonomy in their position when they aren't willing to offer it to their own team members. The key seems to be in keeping them in outside training. Keep them learning and growing.

Level 3 might need managing as well, but that managing has to go up the ladder. It requires great strategy. This would happen if level 2 sees a flaw in the leadership of level 3 and seeks to guide their boss to a different solution or way of thinking.

This can be a risky undertaking. It is best to know the communication style and receiving style of the leader before this is attempted. Principle 5 will cover this in detail.

Though most traditionalists are in level one, a few are still in levels 2 and 3. They need to be herded carefully as they can usually see through personal and company agendas.

Company Pyramid

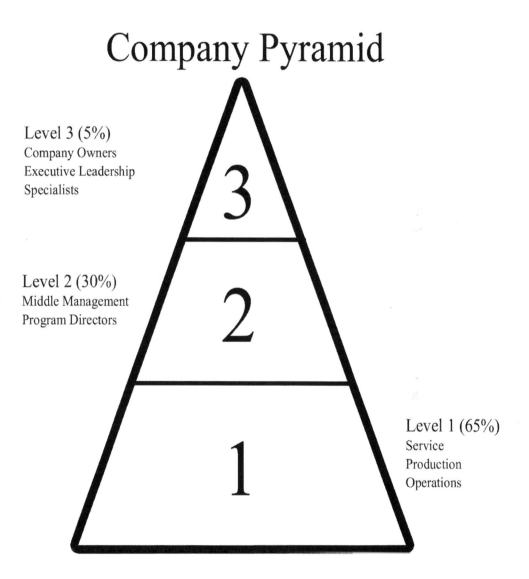

Level 3 (5%)
Company Owners
Executive Leadership
Specialists

Level 2 (30%)
Middle Management
Program Directors

Level 1 (65%)
Service
Production
Operations

Baby Boomers (1946–1963)

Baby Boomers are predominately in their 50s and 60s. They are well-established in their careers and hold positions of power and authority. This generation holds the majority of wealth in the nation and weld tremendous buying power. That fact alone commands them respect. This generation is seeing the greatest changes.

Labor statistics indicate that nearly 80 million Baby Boomers will exit the workplace in the next decade. These employees are retiring at the rate of 8,000 per day or more than 300 per hour. This unprecedented loss of skilled labor in many professions is having dramatic impact.

Baby Boomers are associated with a rejection or redefinition of traditional values. Boomers were widely associated with privilege, as many grew up in a time of widespread government subsidies in post-war housing and education.

As a group, they were the wealthiest, most active, and most physically fit generation to that time. They were the first generation to grow up genuinely expecting the world to improve with time.

Another feature of the Boomers is that they tend to think of themselves as a special generation. They were the first to be studied and defined.

Seventy-six million American children were born in the Baby Boomer generation. They grew up in a time of dramatic social change. There is a distinct divide between those that embrace social change and the more conservative. This is seen in the nearly equal split in alignment with political parties.

The Baby Boomers found that their music, most notably, rock and roll, was another way of expressing the generational identity. They were the first generation to grow up with television.

When we look at herding this generation, the issue of independence comes into play. They are often accused of leading by example rather than by teaching.

"I do not wear my emotions on my sleeve.
I was once described by my own son, Stephen,
as an emotional ostrich!"

- Pierre Salinger

BABY BOOMERS SUMMARY

- Predominately in their 50s and 60s

- Hold the majority of the nation's wealth

- They are retiring at unprecedented rates

- They were the first generation to be studied

- They were the first to have television

- They are accused of being poor delegators

Get your head out of the sand!

List the names of your Baby Boomer team members. When was the last time you gave them a new assignment, and what new skills did they gain from that assignment?

Name: Date Assigned/Skills

1._____   _____

2._____   _____

3._____   _____

4._____   _____

5._____   _____

6._____   _____

7._____   _____

8._____   _____

9._____   _____

10._____   _____

Stop running in circles!

One of the main reasons that team members are not promoted is because they perform tasks that no one else can. Everyone should be training a replacement. To make your work exclusive is career suicide.

HERDING SKILL: DELEGATION

Delegation is an art. It is an art that has changed. At one time it was only about getting things accomplished. Today, it's more complex.

There is a greater expectation for supervisors to meet bottom line budgets and to invest time into the development of their team members.

The first thing that a supervisor should factor in is the pay level of each team member. There would be exceptions here if the company or organization has equalized compensation or are required to match job responsibilities to rank and pay.

First, list every team member in order from highest compensation to lowest. Then, list all of the responsibilities of your department. Finally, check off every team member that is capable of or have the skill set necessary to perform the tasks.

Then, assign the tasks to the level at which they can be accomplished for the least amount of dollars.

Let's begin with entry level. We need to fill their schedule first. There are several reasons for this beyond the bottom line.

New team members need to be busy, and busy quickly. If we don't acclimate them quickly to a full work schedule, they could fall into bad patterns that are difficult to reverse in the future.

Once we train and equip them to take a complete schedule, we can leave them and go to assign tasks to the person who sits in the level immediately above them. This is the most likely place where you found the work to give to the entry level person. Now, you have to refill this person's work load.

That re-filling would come from the level above them, etc. You do this until you reach the top.

Many companies pay dearly for not properly setting up delegation.

Results of poor delegation:

- Team members are unclear of their job description
- Not all team members are busy. Some have lighter loads and could do more
- The most supportive team member can burn out
- The bottom line fails because we are paying too much for routine tasks (Highly compensated employees are doing tasks that someone at minimal wage could handle)
- We allow for occupational hobbies
- We waste time, therefore money
- Team members become protective of their tasks and make it difficult to shift their schedules
- Team members develop a feeling that if they finish their routine tasks, they are free to roam and or leave
- Team members confuse job security with position security
- Position security can cost team members promotions
- The team is not cross-trained
- Crises can occur if a team member is out of the office and no one else can perform his/her task
- Team members are not developing new skills

Results of great delegation:

- Team members are cross-trained

- Team members are equipped to handle crises that arise because some-one else has probably had that assignment in the past

- Team members are advancing the ladder of skill and rank

- Team members are all training their replacement allowing for upward mobility

- Team members fully accept the last line in their job descriptions. Name-ly, "other duties assigned".

- Team members are constantly learning. This leads to high morale, better attendance and a more peaceful work environment

- Every team member respects the job responsibilities of the others in his/her department

- New ideas and solutions come as team members can better understand how operations work

There are some initial challenges to switching to this delegation model. There will be resistance. It would be wise for you as a supervisor to make sure that you have the buy-in from upper management before you begin. (Hint: show them the bottom-line results that you expect to achieve)

You will need to know that if a member of your team attempts to go over your head to challenge the change in their responsibilities that upper man-agement is going to back you. If they do not, the whole system will break down.

There might be a temporary drop in production as training has to occur. This will have its payback in the end.

Team members might not catch on to their benefits immediately. They may suspect that this is a way to simply get more work out of them. One-on-one conversations are going to be important to get their buy-in.

One suggestion might be to post the job skills and responsibilities of the department. As they add a new skill, advance them on the company web-site or bulletin board. They will enjoy seeing their skill list grow and this system might encourage a healthy competition.

Emphasis their growth potential. Teach them the importance of being cross-trained to advance in salary, ranking and respect. Tell them what happens when people lock themselves in and refuse to grow. They will probably be passed over for promotions and be dispensable.

This is one of their greatest misunderstands. Some team members think that if they are the only person who can perform certain task(s), that they are secure in their job. Not so. It is actually the opposite. I have been in many staff meeting discussions to see people passed over for a promotion simply because no one else could cover their duties if they were advanced. What a mess!

Great delegators are on their feet most of the day. You will be managing by walk around. This gives you a better feel of operations and makes you accessible. With the Ostrich delegation model, you will free up time for walking around as you will be moving work off your desk onto the desk of the person that you are training to take your place.

This does not mean that you can put your feet up and pull out the Sudoku puzzles. It means that you can now use your extra time to do three important things for your career:

1. Get more training for yourself.

2. Counsel and coach your team one-on-one which lowers turnover and raises employee morale.

3. Going to your superiors to ask to take on more challenging work. In other words, taking work off their desk.

I call this last one, "Climbing the corporate ladder on the back side while no one is watching". You cross-train yourself into promotions.

Two cautions.

1. If you answer to a micro-manager, they might not allow you to take any work from their desk. They might fear that you are after their job. In this case, the best thing to do is to fill your hours freed by effective delegation with more development and solution projects. Send your ideas over the head of your micro-manager. That can get you noticed from above without appearing to be a direct threat to your immediate supervisor. If this isn't handled properly, you could potentially work yourself out of a job.

2. Be prepared for this as well. If you take work from your bosses' desk, and they do not wisely go to refill their work load from above, they may become more social and absent. This is not always a bad thing. You become the go-to person. Suddenly, you are making the decisions. I call this "achieving results without authority". That is one of my favorite business phrases. Your immediate boss may quit. This could be a result of your inadvertent removal of their sense of purpose at the company. They may not even realize why they suddenly feel as if they have topped out or need another job with more challenge.

Either way, there is a win for you and your entire team.

Delegation Model

Wage	A	B	C	D	E	F
Susan ($30)	X	X	X	X	X	X
Brian ($28)	X	X		X	X	X
David ($25)	X	X			X	X
Lisa ($20)	X				X	X
Tom ($15)					X	X
Kelly ($11)						X

1. Line up all tasks for your department (A-F)
2. Line up team by wage.
3. Assess skill levels.
4. Train into skills not yet developed.
5. Move assignments down once mastered by one.
6. Train Susan to replace you.
7. Fill Kelly's schedule quickly.

GEN X (1964–1982)

This generation marks the period of birth decline after the baby boom and is significantly smaller than previous and succeeding generations. Members of Generation X are largely in the 30s and 40s.

On the whole, they are more ethnically diverse and better educated than the Baby Boomers. Over 60% of Generation X attended college.

Generation X came of age in an era of two-income families, rising divorce rates and a faltering economy. Women were joining the workforce in large numbers, spawning an age of "latch-key" children.

As a result, Generation X is independent, resourceful and self-sufficient. In the workplace, Generation X values freedom and responsibility. Many in this generation display a casual disdain for authority and structured work hours. They dislike being micro-managed and embrace a hands-off management philosophy.

The Generation X mentality reflects a shift from a manufacturing economy to a service economy. They are the first generation to grow up with computers and much of our current technology. This generation is comfortable using PDAs, cell phones, email, laptops, Blackberrys and other technology tools.

Many Gen Xers lived through tough economic times in the 1980s and saw their workaholoic parents lose hard-earned positions. Thus, Generation X is less committed to one employer and is more willing to change jobs to get ahead than previous generations. They adapt well to change. Generation X is ambitious and eager to learn new skills but want to accomplish things on their own terms.

Unlike previous generations, members of Generation X work to live rather than live to work. They appreciate fun in the workplace and espouse a work hard/play hard mentality. Generation X managers often incorporate humor and games into work activities.

GEN X
SUMMARY

- In their 30s and 40s

- Ethnically diverse

- Educated

- 60% attended college

- Independent

- Resourceful

- Values freedom

- Values responsibility

- Disdain for authority

- Do not like structured work hours

- Dislike being micro-managed

- Strongly dislike meetings

Get your head out of the sand!

Look at your last meeting agenda. List the topics on it. How much time was allotted going into the meeting? Which items were finished; which were tabled for future discussion?

Item: Time: Completed?

1. _____   _____   _____

2. _____   _____   _____

3. _____   _____   _____

4. _____   _____   _____

5. _____   _____   _____

6. _____   _____   _____

7. _____   _____   _____

8. _____   _____   _____

9. _____   _____   _____

10. _____

Stop running in circles!

Most companies have no idea how to run an effective meeting. Meetings are often expensive, a source of disappointment, a breeding point of negativity as well as for groupthink and bullying. Generation X sees meetings as an unnecessary evil.

"As the ostrich when pursued hideth his head,
but forgetting his body; so the fears of a coward
expose him to danger."

- King of Egypt, 14th Century B.C.E.

HERDING SKILL:
EFFECTIVE MEETINGS

G eneration X is not fond of meetings. Sitting still and being compliant is not their thing. They want instant solutions for problems. Sitting in a meeting with them feels like sitting with a kindergarten class. They wiggle and make their impatience known with tapping of feet and thumping of pencils.

With every problem, it seems as if they automatically ask if there is a website, App, or software program that might solve it. This is not to imply that they are lazy or lacking creativity. When inspired they are both tireless laborers and highly creative.

Meetings are consistently on their list of unnecessary time and money wasters. Meetings are meant to save or create healthy bottom lines, but Xers see that they often go in the other direction.

Meetings are either informative or creative/problem-solving in nature. There isn't much that can be done to make informative meetings exciting.

It would be smart for meeting leaders not to mix an informative meeting agenda into one that is also meant to be creative. An analytical lead-in such as updates of company benefits or details of an upcoming company picnic can kill creativity.

If a meeting must be a combination of informative and creative, an activity that could help attendees to "flip" to the side of the brain (creative to analytical) when it is called for by the schedule.

For example, if a meeting starts with an analytical topic, it would be wise to add a creative activity before switching to creative topics. There are many books and web-sites in which to find creative activities for this purpose.

On the other hand, if the meeting starts in creative mode and needs to wrap in analytical, it would be wise to include an activity to help your team to flip back. Solving Math problems would one idea.

To get Xers excited about a creative or problem-solving meeting, it is important to build the right framework. Try to stay clear of words like "meeting" and "agenda". They are not likely to spawn enthusiasm.

Consider setting up your meetings as an event. Write the agenda as a program outline. Give the event an intriguing title. A sample program outline is given at the end of this section.

For our example we used the title "Generation Y vs. Acme". The meeting is going to focus on the effective marketing of our newest video game. Generation Y is our target market and Acme is our company name.

After the title, we give the logistics of the meeting; who, where, when, and a sentence that instructs them to bring this one-sheet with them. For the first event that you hold, distribute the program one-sheet just as we suggest in our example. Give no further details or explanations.

As you are intending to keep your meeting focused and positives for the Xers, set a tight schedule and specific segments. After you list the amount of time to be allotted to each segment, include a brief description of the discussion that is to occur. Too much time is wasted in meetings by informing everyone of the problem once they have arrived. Even if they were given a topic on an agenda, participants are often in the dark as to the details. They come unprepared to solve it.

In the example that we provided, there are three segments with titles and an explanation of our challenge. Twenty minutes are allotted to each segment. There are blank lines under each segment to encourage the team to come armed with solutions. One side asks for potential solutions, the other asks for the source of the idea. No other instructions are given.

When the program begins, you welcome the group with enthusiasm. You start quickly with the announcement that the meeting is now focusing on the first of the three concerns. You are specific that it is the only topic on the floor for the next 20 minutes. (I find it effective to run a count-down timer on my presentation screen that sounds an alarm when the 20 minutes is up.)

It is likely that your one-sheet will be ignored by most attendees. It is also likely that some team members will come prepared. You probably know who on your team will be prepared. As you are starting your opening remarks, walk towards the most likely prepared member of your team and see if their sheet is present and filled out. If it is, begin with them. "Jennifer, I see that you have something there, so why don't you kick us off with your thoughts on this topic.

Notice what you just accomplished there. You have effectively turned over the meeting floor to your positive, prepared team member. The naysayers can't get in. They are blocked.

After Jennifer finishes, be sure to acknowledge her efforts and preparedness. Praise her for the source of her idea, whether she researched it or created the solution herself.

Here is the only point where a negative person can take the floor from you and the problem-solvers. They might attempt to interject their thoughts that Jennifer's idea is not feasible and won't solve anything. Move towards the dissenter and with complete respect say something like, "Ben that is exactly what we need here, an open sharing of ideas. Why don't you go ahead and share what you came up with."

You can expect that Ben has absolutely nothing in front of him. He is probably not prepared. He will most likely be defensive. Again, with respect, tell him that you look forward to hearing his thoughts on this at the next meeting. Holding strong eye contact, ask him directly if he can have his idea ready for that meeting. Stay silent until he answers. Then, move away. You have just set the ground rules for your meetings. Be prepared or be quiet.

Let's say for the sake of argument, Ben is prepared when he took shots at Jennifer's solution. Great! He now puts his solution on the floor and you proceed with comparing Ben's solution with Jennifer's. Now you are running an effective, creative meeting. Continue through the three concerns in the same manner.

It is highly unlikely that any of your three topics will be resolved within 20 minutes. All will be carried over to the next meeting. This is not a problem. You really don't want to solve the problem today. Most team members were not prepared. You do not have enough perspectives represented.

You will find a considerable increase in the percentage of team members that come prepared to the next event. You will want to increase the amount of time that you allot to the three concerns. Your numbers will likely increase from 5% prepared for the first event to nearly 40% prepared for the second event.

By the third or fourth event, your numbers could hit close to 100%. One way to ensure that they do is to make the events voluntary. After team members experience the excitement and effectiveness of your events, they will know if they want to participate going forward.

Not everyone enjoys this part of the process. They shouldn't be forced to attend. Many analyticals prefer to build the systems after the direction has been set. Forcing them to attend the "what if" part of the process is inviting negativity. Let them remain focused on what they do best. Everyone will be happier. One final suggestion is to be clear that those who do not attend the event cannot complain about the decisions later.

One of the great outcomes of this system is the increased research that will be done by your team. As they begin to compete for the floor, they will direct more time and mental energy to finding solutions.

As often happens, when you find a solution to one problem, it might create another. In this case, you might find yourself with a 90%-100% participation and struggle to get every idea on to the floor. You do not want to run your meetings over two hours. You might have to ask your team to turn in their ideas 48 hours in advance. You can then organize and group the ideas to create a new one-sheet for the meeting. For example, if six team members suggest red for the color of the cover, you can list the idea and the six that suggested it and allow them open floor to share their reasoning.

You have now reached your goal for meetings. Team members are presented with company challenges, they strategize solutions, they hand them to you in advance, and you conduct an effective meeting. This will surely help in herding Xers into the team.

SAMPLE MEETING SHEET

Generation Y vs. AMEX
Friday, September 15, 2012
Conference Room B
1:00-2:00 PM
[Bring this Sheet with You]

1:00-1:20   RESULTS OF GEN Y SURVEYS

We just received the results from our study group on our latest video game. Our game is testing well in most areas. There was some negative feedback in two areas. Some Generation Y members of the study group found the box cover to be forgettable and reported that the game did not move quickly enough to hold their interest on level one.

Your ideas: Source of your idea:

_____   _____

_____   _____

_____   _____

1:20-1:40   COMPETITION

Our competitors, Braxton, also tested their game this month. Their feedback is much like ours. However, their box design scored higher. They had the same challenge with their game moving slowly in level one.

Your ideas: Source of your idea:

_____   _____

_____   _____

_____   _____

1:40-2:00   EXECUTION

Braxton is set to introduce their new game on December 1 in time for the Christmas holiday season. They intend to release the game without attempting to improve the game speed. Should we do the same, or allow them to take their game to the public first and wait until March to release our game. This would give us a chance to watch the receptiveness of the consumer.

Your ideas: Source of your idea:

_____   _____

_____   _____

_____   _____

MILLENNIALS (1982–1998)

Generations, like people, have personalities, and Millennials, the American teens and twenty-somethings who are making the passage into adulthood at the start of a new millennium have begun to forge theirs. They are confident, self-expressive, liberal, upbeat and open to change.

They are more ethnically and racially diverse than older adults. They're less religious, less likely to have served in the military, and are on track to become the most educated generation in American history.

Their entry into careers and first jobs has been badly set back by the Great Recession, but they are more upbeat than their elders about their own economical future as well as about the overall state of the union.

Millennials are global thinkers. They are fans of programs that make the world a better place in their opinion, like conservation.

They embrace multiple modes of self-expression. Three-quarters have created a profile on a social networking site. One-in-five have posted a video of themselves online. Nearly four-in-ten have a tattoo and one-in-four has a piercing. This might cause many companies to re-visit their policies of professional dress code. Once the Millennials become the prime consumer (currently a female Baby Boomer), the accepted appearance of the company representative changes.

Their look-at-me tendencies are not without limits. Most Millennials have placed privacy boundaries on their social media profiles. And 70% say their tattoos are hidden beneath clothing.

Despite struggling (and often failing) to find jobs in the recession, about nine-in-ten either say that they currently have enough money or that they will eventually meet their long-term financial goals. But at the moment, fully 37% of 18-29-year-olds are unemployed or out of the workforce, the highest share among this age group in more than three decades. We do not know if this reflects a positive attitude towards their lives, or indicates that they are still relying on their parents for financial security.

Millennials are on course to become the most educated generation in American history, a trend driven largely by the demands of a modern knowledge-based economy, but most likely accelerated by their inability to find a job.

They respect their elders. A majority say that the older generation is superior to the younger generation when it comes to moral values and work ethic. The older the generation, the greater the respect offered up.

"He behaved like an ostrich and put his head in the sand thereby exposing his thinking parts."

- George Carman

MILLENNIALS SUMMARY

- Like working in teams only if individuality is allowed

- Sometimes referred to as Generation Y

- Quickly becoming the most educated generation

- Quickly becoming the spending generation

- Distrust research

- Loyal to brands

- Lose their trust, and it is almost impossible to rebuild

- See their career in 4-year increments

- Strongly focused on self-development

- Their desire for fast, easy answers gets them labeled as lazy

- Constantly ask "why"

- Don't like being boxed in

Get your head out of the sand!

Millennials are sharp cookies. In an interview process, they are actually interviewing you and your company. They are clever enough to work it so that you are probably not seeing it. They will focus on what they can gain from you to help them in their future goals. This is not necessarily a bad thing. They will meet you half way once they are on the team. They are inquisitive and like to solve problems. Even if this group is the one to declare that "career planning is an oxymoron", they are willing to give you four great years.

Stop running in circles!

Companies might benefit themselves if they were to spend more time examining a potential or current employee's resume and career objectives than their time cards. Motivating factors for Millennials is desire to achieve and hope of gain, not fear of loss. With them, the art of discipline is really the art of development.

"A writer may tell me he thinks man will ultimately become an ostrich. I cannot properly contradict him."

- Thomas Malthus

HERDING SKILL:
INTERVIEWING & HIRING

Millennials are professional interviewers. They can go on line and look up the job for which they are interviewing and be given tips and sample questions that they can expect. They are well-schooled when they walk through your company doors. Add to that the complexity of checking references today and the result is often a misplaced hire.

One effective way to get to the core of what you have in front of you in an interview process is to give the candidate some homework.

The Ostrich approach to interviewing offers clarity for the interviewer. When potential employees come to apply for a job with your company, collect the necessary data and call them back for a second interview. Call all of them back for a second interview. The reason that I advise calling all of them back is to get beyond the often-misleading first impression. People are often beaten down by the interview process. The best of them will show once they see that they were worthy of a call-back.

After setting the second interview date and time, ask the interviewee to bring a 100-day action plan with them on that day. Explain to them that you are looking for their vision of their potential contributions and their focus in the first three months on the team. Our numbers show that up to 75% of people will cancel their second interview when you ask them for the home-work.

We don't know why that number is so high, but we can imagine. This probably eliminates the minimalists, the disinterested, the unskilled, the uninformed and the uninspired. We won't have to waste anyone's time and we get solid candidates.

A smart interviewee will research your company, your product or service, and your competition. They might ask for or at least assume that they know the challenges that your company is facing. From that, they will build an action plan that boldly addresses the challenges. Their creativity and contributions will be evident. It's hard to fake your way through this process. How wonderful for you to expand positions with new ideas through interviews.

GENERATION FLUX

With our visibility of the future declining, a group of American workers has separated themselves from the pack. FastCompany profiled this group in their February, 2012 magazine, assigning them the name of Generation Flux.

They are breaking out as a result of their frustration with the slow pace of big corporations to keep up with change. They think such companies are too slow and not innovating quickly enough.

Fluxers believe that there's a need to be less hierarchical and to rely more on teams. However, they are also redefining teams. They are individualistic in team approach. Principle 2 goes deeper into team building.

Fluxers are looking for opportunities to gather new information and tools to help them get where they are going. Their resumes are all over the place, and they are proud of that fact. They believe that a diverse work history is as valuable as a liberal arts degree; it says that they have been open to opportunity.

You do not have to be a jack-of-all-trades to flourish in the age of flux, but you do need to be open-minded. Rigid work schedules and requirements for physical appearance are not going to draw them into your company.

We have to give them credit for one thing. They are determinedly resilient. They are attempting to create order in a chaotic world.

This generation may well settle back into their prescribed age generation within a few short years when the next generation enters the workforce. Only time will show the impact of this brave and innovative group upon the survival of business.

FLUX GENERATION SUMMARY

- Can come be of any age, no limitations

- Impatient with slow moving corporate pace

- Highly innovative

- Like to use technology to solve problems

- Drawn to master-mind groups

- Want to work when in creative mode

- Dislike structure and authority

- Always looking for the next big idea

Get your head out of the sand!

Does your company have a viable recognition and rewards system in place to encourage the sharing of ideas? Is it working? Do team members trust it? Are you encouraging study and education on company time that will lead to solutions and innovation?

Take a few minutes to design a system of recognition and rewards that your company can afford and one that will get immediate action.

_____

_____

_____

_____

_____

_____

_____

_____

_____

List some rewards you can offer.

_____

_____

_____

_____

_____

_____

_____

_____

_____

_____

_____

_____

_____

Stop running in circles!

Fluxers do not want to be micro-managed. In fact, they will flat out refuse it. You would probably be getting in the way of some unfathomable creativity anyway. They are focused and determined. They do like for you to listen to and support their ideas. That is the most you will get from them in the form of dependence.

Their idea of being rewarded is usually through dollars invested in them and their ideas. They also like to be given the freedom of time to develop their ideas. They want you to trust them. Don't try to push your way into this group. You must wait to be invited. If you do receive the coveted invite, come prepared with your plan to change the world as we know it.

HERDING SKILL: REWARDING NEW IDEAS

Ideas are breeding in the minds of your team. If you were careful to hire the right people, there are probably hundreds of ideas sitting in your cubicles right now.

The younger generations respect the older ones, but still have an underlying distrust that their ideas will be credited to them.

Any company operating today without a solid ideas-generating system will likely be gone within the next five years.

The Ostrich system works on the theory that people want money for their ideas. It doesn't have to be millions, but it does have to be cash. Recognition lacks luster with fluxers. They are incentivized by the "show me the money" results.

Companies would be wise to set up internal links to store and reward idea sharing. It cannot sit idle. When ideas come in, there should be instant gratification. Meaning, any idea that is offered to directly affect the bottom line should be rewarded. Imagine if companies offered a $25.00 cash reward the very week that an original idea is submitted. Even if the idea does not make it to the implementation stage, this could keep the ideas flowing.

Your creative employee walking around without an outlet for his or her idea and at the same time in need of some extra spending cash or wanting to add to their savings, will get on to the site to get busy. It's a win-win.

This could be the way to finally get the entire team into a daily problem-solving state of mind. Ideas that make it past the first level and are referred to an operations committee could be rewarded with a higher cash reward. Ideas that are eventually implemented could be in the form of profit-sharing or a buy-out. Do that, and you will have a very motivated team.

"Ostriches are more practical than they are given credit for.
They do not stick their heads in the sand to disappear,
they are seeking water for survival.
They have not survived for millions of years by hiding."

- Anonymous

Nexters (1999–)

They're here! The new generation. They have yet to be named. We refer to them here as Nexters.

This generation is going to shake the game up again, and they are also going to reverse some of it. The term "Nexters" signifies a new beginning for this generation. I doubt that many Americans would argue that we need a new beginning.

There is a grassroots belief that we also need to recapture some of the values and practices that made this country great.

Gen Next is going to do all of these things.

The Gen Nexters were toddlers or yet-to-be-born when terrorists attacked on US soil. (9/11/2001) The effects of that horrific day were felt around the globe. It is still causing aftershocks for our nation.

This 14-and-younger generation has seen war as a reality. That has caused them to be cautionary. They are less concerned about international affairs than the preceding Millennial generation. It's hard to fault them. We cannot imagine what the world looks like from their perspective. They see soldiers on TV and walking past them on the streets and in the airports. They hear about financial challenges and lost jobs and homes over dinner. Many have lived or are living through those things themselves.

I have a special concern for this generation. I think that they will be misread. I can see where their quiet demeanors and disciplined decision-making will cause other generations to think that they are content when there is much bubbling under the surface.

Until now, most concern has been upon the outcome of the Millennial generation. There is talk of their sense of entitlement, their lack of being in touch with reality, and their push-back from leadership. I am not one of those concerned. Millennials are dreamers. Dreamers are always fine. Yes, they will get their bubbles burst a few times, but they are equipped with the right stuff to get up again. They will be fine.

I worry about the Gen Nexters. They are not dreaming. Only one-in-three of them see themselves see higher education in their future. The main reason given is the expense. These children and teens are familiar with student loans and they are cautious to create debt.

Their instinctual lack of trust due to international affairs and a bust economy has caused them to go internal and to be more self-reliant. This will make it difficult for us to corral them into an effective/trusting team.

If they are not supported in their dreaming of a better future, we might end up with a poverty mentality in our nation. We might see less emphasis on the STEM programs that keep us competitive internationally. (Science, Technology, Engineering, and Math) The United States already ranks at 22 in Math and 23 in Science as compared to other nations. Evidently, wealth is not the motivator. Apparently, neither is accessibility.

I borrowed this statement from my son Steven. "The three indisputable things necessary for education to occur are fascination, determination, and opportunity."

This generation is going to need motivation and positive feedback to step out of their comfort zones. Their workplace will also need to do their part to promote higher education and training. Much of this might be done at the company's expense. There may be a rise in the dollars for scholarship programs such as the one offered by the Chick-fil-a Corporation.

Some companies may have to introduce global awareness programs if one of their goals is to operate or to sell outside of the U.S. Gen Next might not care about international affairs as much as we need them to. They are focused on the poverty they see in their neighborhoods and the natural disasters that keep taking a toll on their fellow Americans.

NEXTERS SUMMARY

- Born just prior to or following the 9/11 terrorist attacks in the U.S.

- Less likely to be global-minded than Millennials

- More concerned about domestic needs of their own country

- Financially responsible

- Less likely to take risks

- Aligned with the Traditionalists in their thinking

- Carrying traditional values into a non-traditional world

- Their instinct cautious trust will challenge us in integrating them into a team

Get your head out of the sand!

Gen Next may well revive motivational speaking. (My fellow speakers just sat up in their chairs.)

This generation will need to be shown how to dream big again. They will need to learn to put down their guards and to trust others to have their best interest at heart. The best way to help them to that place is to integrate them into company and out-of-the company networking systems. There are many great groups that offer this in your community.

Gen next will probably feel more comfortable sharing their ideas and concerns initially with outsiders. Once they feel validated, they will return to you with their ideas in hand.

Invest wisely in their networking. It will return ten-fold.

Stop running in circles!

Leaders have four years to prepare their new coaching skills. Gen Next is going to need intense focus from their companies to generate ideas. This is not because they lack creativity, but rather because there are instinctively drawn into themselves for solutions. They lack trust. We will have to pull our cheerleader uniforms back out of the attics (hoping that they still fit), and bring back good old-fashioned "you can do it" support. Building their trust will probably begin outside of our companies.

HERDING SKILL: NETWORKING & LIBRARIES

For this generation, we have listed two separate ideas to keep them herding with your team. First, get them active in networking groups. Second, get them to build learning libraries of study.

1.   List the networking groups and alliances within your community. Note the date and times that they meet.

Name	Day	Time
_____	_____	_____
_____	_____	_____
_____	_____	_____
_____	_____	_____
_____	_____	_____

2.   List the publications/journals/web-sites that address the challenges of your industry. Trade magazines are available in print and on-line.

Name of site/publication   Area of focus   Cost

_____   _____   _____

_____   _____   _____

_____   _____   _____

_____   _____   _____

_____   _____   _____

Start with networking. Once you have done the research of groups meeting in your community, ask your Gen next members to choose the ones that spike their interest. Sign them up for the memberships. Pay their fees. Expect them to attend on the company time and expense. Expect them to share the information that they gain. This will start their networking system.

Teach them effective networking.

The Ostrich system of networking encourages the team member to collect business cards (contact information) rather than give out theirs. Giving out cards is usually pointless. Not many people take this form of networking seriously. Most of us collect cards, don't look at them until we are cleaning out our jackets, purses, and briefcases and putting them into a drawer. We usually don't see them again until we are throwing the drawer of cards into the trash.

When networking, Gen Nexters should treat business cards as the great networking tool that they were meant to be. Hold attention on the person as they speak. Use all the tactics you were taught to remember them and to be remembered. Be actively collecting information. Once the other person walks away, take a minute to turn over the business card, jot down notes to recall the person. Specifically, jot down details of their job, their appearance, the date and event where you met them and something that will allow you to mark correspondence with them as confidential. This is not as hard as it sounds. If someone tells you that they are seeking a promotion, a company move, a career decision, were recently promoted or even shared some personal information, this makes the letter and/or email confidential.

Give them a score of 1 or 2. Now, put the card away and move on. After returning from a networking event, go over the cards with them. Decide first what is to be done with the 1s. These were people that your Gen Next team member did not deem as a strong connection. Still, send them a professional email the day after the event. You never know when they see more in the connection and want to follow up with you.

The 2s are more critical. Your Gen Next team member sensed something in this person that might add to their career or to your company. They will get a professional hand-written note on company letterhead. The letter is short. It just expresses the appreciation of the introduction, the recognition of the confidential information shared, a note of encouragement, and an expressed desire to continue the professional relationship.

These are highly affective networking tactics. Especially, when they are hand-written and hand-address envelopes marked "confidential". Help your Gen next set up a tickler system to stay in touch with their new contacts.

The second herding skill here is in building learning libraries. Gen next needs information and they need it quickly to stay competitive with the fluxers and Millennials preceding them.

After they select their journals/sites, have them collect at least three articles from each on a monthly or weekly basis. These articles are usually designed to be 15-minute reads. This is a direct result of our shortened attention spans.

Allow (even require) your Gen Next team members to read one article a day on company time. Have them discuss what they learn. If there is a solid idea to share, have them write a memo and distribute it to the team. Have them speak on the articles at company meetings.

Meet with your Gen Next people as time allows and support their efforts. I liken this to "reading with the Principal" time at school. It is going to have a big impact on them as you work towards a healthier workplace.

The journey has just started! Use the information you have learned about the generations to start really having a great time getting to know your team.

Principle Two

There are Two Types of Teams, Not One!

I became aware that there are two types of teams in high school. In the same season, I was on the gymnastics team and the basketball team. The difference in these two types of teams was evident from the selection process through the training and practice sessions.

One (gymnastics) was based on individual performance for the overall good, and the other (basketball) was based on a pass-pass success formula.

As soon as you read that sentence, it should have been obvious to you as to which team you best fit. Your career from this day forward should be designed to keep you on the right type of team for your talents. You will be miserable playing on the wrong one.

Team-building books and speaker programs have largely been educating us on creating successful Type 1 (pass-pass) team. There is talk of equal reward and incentive programs that include everyone. Type 2 (individual performers) isn't biting.

The individual performers of Type 2 like to spar with their teammates. They will share ideas that will put the company team in top position, but they are well aware that they are also competing with their teammates.

These players are put into the precarious situation of sharing ideas that will help the team to win without giving up the ideas that will ensure that they remain the top dog. They are the gymnasts. Put a gymnast-mentality on a basketball team and everyone is miserable. The same is true the other way around.

In the workplace, the pass-pass team will focus on excellence from all members in their areas of expertise with an understanding of what the other team members will need from them. Each player expects to be able to hand off their part of the project to the next player when their part of the process is finished. This would be like a surgical team. There is no room for the competitive individual performer on that type of team. Someone might get hurt and certainly performance can be affected.

A sales team would be one example of the individual performance team. They do well when there is a competition among the team. Each will push harder to be at the top. This will elevate the entire company.

Most Millennials and Fluxers (and a portion of the Xers) are individual performers. They are more gymnastics rather than basketball mentality. This is the core reason that most team incentive programs are failing to connect. Attendance at company picnics and department birthday parties is not what it once used to be.

Here is the critical part for companies to recognize. It is also these individual performers that are probably walking around with the next big idea in their head. Would we really want to lose them to the competition over a rigid management style?

I know this is not going to be easy to work with, but it is possible. Corporate America didn't always have time clocks. It is going to be sticking point for future hires. I heard it from a Millennial in class as we discussed the importance of on-time arrival at work. "As I see it, your generation is way too hung up on 180 seconds; you guys need to get over it. Results are the main thing, It would be counter-productive to replace top talent over six minutes of time, but that is what most policy manuals would dictate."

His comment wasn't meant to be rude. His tone was calm and he was smiling. He was just calling it as he saw it. He firmly believes that if he stays late, works through lunch and finishes his projects, then he is doing everything that is expected of him and more. He is not alone in his thinking.

One company that I consulted with in Atlanta had a challenge with tardiness.

Their team was comprised of mostly Millennials. They were frustrated, but found a solution. They allowed the team members to choose their starting time of 7:00, 7:30, 8:00 or 8:30. Once they chose their time, however, they were locked-in for six months and would be subject to the company's discipline policy on tardiness. After six months, they could re-set their starting time. The company's tardiness problem was pretty much over. It seemed that the employees just wanted to be included in the process.

The time clock isn't only a problem at starting time. If forced to stop work at certain times or to attend meetings and company functions, the creative process of an individual team player can be affected in a negative way. Open time clocks may be the way for some companies to succeed.

I visited a software-development company owned by a friend in Atlanta. He told me that he had 120 employees and he wanted me to come to take a tour.

We started with a reception in the main lobby of his building. It was pretty evident that not all 120 people were in attendance.

After the reception, Scott gave me a tour. We ended up on a side of the building that was separated by a long hallway. As we stood outside a wide set of doors, he asked if I could hold any conversation and questions until we had gotten to the other side of this room.

When he opened the doors, the best way to describe what I saw was a giant dorm room. There were no walls or cubicles. There were sleeping bags, empty pizza boxes, and jackets on the floor. There were 60 desks, 60 computers, and 60 people. Here was the rest of the team.

The men and women were data processors and software designers. They didn't seem to be aware that we had entered the room. There was little to no conversation going on. They did not even look up to acknowledge their boss. When Scott and I exited on the other side, he joked that they pretty much leave those guys alone. He said that they occasionally drop pizza by and send in cleaning crews. That's it. They were allowed to come and go as they liked. They could work any hours they chose. They could work around the clock for days and then take off for days. Scott shared with me that a study of their time at their computer stations backed that they actually worked 20% more hours than required of them. He supported their creative process and didn't want to interrupt it.

That may sound like a new innovative international company that you have read about. But, the year of my visit was 1999. Scott was ahead of his time. He is a visionary. He hired the right people and got out of their way. He also sold that company about three months after that day for over 94 million dollars. I imagine that the software developers enjoyed their stock monies as much as they enjoyed their jobs.

This is one example of how we will have to be creative to keep the two teams incentivized in the future. The challenges here will come in keeping us out of legal entanglement if we individualize rules. That will be the responsibility of the leadership and the human resource departments.

It will be smart to interview for positions with a clear understanding as which type of team mentality is needed. The right questions will ensure that you get the right player in the right sport. A mixed team mentality is rarely successful.

"It takes courage to be a dove. Honor accrues to the ostrich."

- Anonymous

Principle Three

*"Those who don't know history
are destined to repeat it."*

- Edmund Burke

The Next Generation could sink or save us! Seth Johnson will be writing the following section about this all-important principle.

I became familiar with Seth Johnson's work on social emotional development at a leadership development program in Boston in 2005. It was hard not to notice him in a room of strategists. He was constantly questioning common thinking on leadership and the true motivators of employees that are often overlooked.

He was one of those guys that you think you were going to eventually wish would stay quiet, except that everything that he presented made sense and his words silenced the audience.

When Seth boldly stated that poverty could be eliminated from the planet with in two generations and that he had the theories to prove it, I became intrigued.

Seth is the model Millennial. He is global thinking, undeterred from his mission, self-assured, and willing to work impossible hours to prove that he is right.

Over the last seven years, I have been a student of his theories. His writings on adults caught in crimes and poor decisions, told in flash-back form to their childhoods with an explanation of how society set them up to fail are chilling. I have never forgotten one of his stories nor the names of the children. He is a vivid writer.

Seth is a perfect fit to Herding Ostriches as he is a student of history and shows us how society keeps turning in circles and not solving the core problems. The picture of one sticking their heads in the sand and at the same time running in circles is clear in Principle Three.

Mostly, it is my hope that the reader sees how Seth and other Millennials are not going to spend too much time in the past. They are indeed dreamers and hopeful that good things are to come.

The following essay was written entirely by Seth Johnson, and is printed here with his permission.

A Lesson in Business History

Born in 1771, Robert Owens did the unimaginable. So remarkable was his idea, that between 1815 and 1820, twenty thousand people visited New Lanark to witness this modern day conundrum. A successful businessman before the age of 30, his new-age spinning mills were adored by workers and loathed by capitalists. A pioneer in his era, Robert Owens was the first to consider it poor business practice to have 8 year old children work 13 hour shifts.

Not only did he deem it immoral to grind the future of children in his factories, but then he did the inconceivable: he opened a school! The first of its kind, Owens founded a preschool which focused on learning as an enjoyable experience. As well as opening the first adult night school, Owens provided families with clean, respectable housing in safe communities. Furthermore, he stunned capitalists of his time by prohibiting corporal punishment in his factories and retraining managers in humane disciplinary techniques. While his lifelong advocacy for worker's rights did little to persuade other businesses to follow suit, people were truly confounded how a future pioneer in human resource strategies could treat workers admirably, and still make a fortune. (O'Tool, 1995)

Generational leadership is now a reality for success. Herding Ostriches is supporting that reality. Another reality is that though generations change in their needs and desires for their workplace and as customers, there does seem to be a core thread running throughout history.

A man goes to work, the story of life. In medieval times, it may have been a blacksmith or a clergyman. During the birth of America, it could have been a factory worker or fisherman. From the beginning of civilization, it may be a farmer, civil servant, salesman, scholar, or any type of job that you keep today. Even as a Neanderthal, going to work was to hunt and fish. A man goes to work to support his family, the one true constant throughout life.

When considering the generations of workers throughout the centuries, what is the common perception between them all? Before kings ruled the land, and as true today as it ever was, a worker needs to work hard and do what they're told. Depending on their superiors, some people were treated justly, while others were abused to the point of giving their lives. However, throughout wars, famine, and disease, it was the workers who carried civilization to a brighter day.

In the early twentieth century, Elton Mayo had an unprecedented idea. He found that giving textile plant workers occasional rest breaks actually increased productivity! Workers were grateful, the boss was making more profit, and everyone benefitted. Unfortunately when Mayo parted ways with the plant, the residing foremen quashed breaks and productivity plunged back to its original exhaustive level. (Trahair, 2001)

Pioneers before their time, Owens and Mayo paved the way for human resource philosophies by understanding that people's energy, aptitudes, and general well-being are vital resources when creating a successful organization. In the face of animosity, these men were not solely seeking profits, but knowing it was unfair how rival businesses exploited workers, had the morals to respect those that made profit possible. Incidentally, Owens and Mayo stumbled upon a recipe to maximize worker's productivity and thereby increase profits: treat workers admirably, and they work admirably. While Owens dedicated his life to promoting worker's rights, his advocacy was met with fierce resistance. Two hundred years later, how does your job treat you?

Top-Down Idealogies

These historical examples, as I'm sure you have your own, reinforce a centuries-old perception of business organizations: they sacrifice people for profits. Throughout history, the majority of businesses operate with supervisors making decisions and workers following orders. In a militantly ranked, top-down hierarchy, people have little or no control over their work, which creates a dependency on their bosses (Bolman & Deal, 2003). While kings were inherently wealthy, today's businesses are on a continuous quest for profits. Whether ruling with compassion or tyranny, each administration has a substantial effect on the quality of life of its workers.

From kings to CEOs, decisions made at the top of an organization dictate the philosophy of the entire hierarchy. If a CEO manages a business which shares stock, that organization's top priority will be to maximize profit. Because the only reason to purchase stock is to make $, the CEO must make decisions in order to create the most profitable business possible. As superiors dictate to subordinates down the chain, their decisions will also be made in order to fulfill the goals of the company, thereby making it everyone's job to make a profit.

Is one of your responsibilities at work to care about profits? If not, it's certainly a responsibility for your boss, as well as their boss. Rising to the top of the hierarchy, owners need to care about profits; there's no other reason to start a business! Because employees won't work without pay, even nonprofits need to care about the bottom line. It's rarely a good decision to hire a worker for $2 if you're not making $3 from their effort. Without profit, it's not possible to operate a monetarily run organization. While a worker's job is to work, as you climb the supervisor ladder, eventually everyone's obligation turns into caring about profit. Consequently, every one of us has the same boss: profit!

On the contrary, Owens cared about his worker's quality of life. Dictating to subordinates, those goals were also reflected throughout the business. As decisions were made down the hierarchy, managers and workers alike enjoyed their jobs, resulting in a happy, efficient working environment. Satisfied employees are much more productive than those treated poorly, which resulted in additional profit for Owens. The primary goals of an organization, whether for profit or quality of life, directly relate to the well-being of its employees.

Unfortunately, business organizations that have their heads in the sand, do not subscribe to Owen's example of a human resource philosophy. Content workers able to provide for their families are less likely to resent their organization's goals, however workers who feel they are being treated unfairly may form unions that they feel will rebalance power between themselves and management. This power struggle results in less efficient workers, as well as wasting costly time and labor for management. If workers felt as if they were treated fairly, there might not see a need for unions, workers would be more productive, and management would be free to pursue other business matters.

When businesses wield their superiority in the name of profits, workers often become frustrated, directly affecting their productivity. Why work hard so bosses and businessmen can make a profit? Forced to complete boring, tedious tasks, workers become lethargic and apathetic: today is the same as yesterday, tomorrow the same as today. While workers slip into a mind-numbing routine, it's difficult for many owners to admit there's a problem, as long as the business is profitable. Faced with these frustrations, workers often respond by:

- becoming indifferent and apathetic toward their work.

- arriving late, being absent, or quitting altogether.

- limiting productivity through carelessness, deception, or sabotage.

- seeking promotion to a more rewarding position (Bolman & Deal, 2003).

While a worker's prosperity is directly affected by their place of employment, so too are their families. Workers able to properly sustain basic needs may have families and raise children in a stable, nurturing atmosphere. However, disgruntled worker's families are equally affected by their realities. Exhausted from being overworked and underappreciated, it is difficult to raise children in an optimal environment. Workers suffering pay cuts and downsizing may struggle to pay bills, creating more stress in the household. Even more costly, those with little hope to improve their family's circumstances also temper expectations for their children, thereby affecting forthcoming generations of workers.

A New Type of Working Environment

Owens was the first in his time to abolish corporal punishment in his factories, which also means physical punishment was an every day occurrence, even an expected aspect of the working class. A man goes home to his humble castle, tired from excruciating labor and the occasional beating, how would you expect him to treat his family? With little control on the job, many workers likely dominated their families, tyrannizing their children when considered disobedient. With already tempered expectations, children from these families must overcome abhorrent tribulations to have any hope of changing their destiny.

Today, physical punishment is no longer socially acceptable, however similar detrimental working environments plague the next generation. While employees continue to be overworked and underappreciated, modern business organizations have grown to favor a "professional" working environment. The next generation must navigate a new type of managerial style where conflict is often avoided and individuality is suppressed. Eschewing interrelationship problems between coworkers and management builds a distain which reverberates throughout the organization's hierarchy. Melding the classic do-what-you're-told mentality with a "professional" atmosphere, promoting introverted social behaviors, and an underlying tone of anxiety and tension is established.

Like a beaten factory worker tyrannizing his family, a person working in a "professional" environment may also tend to react at home as they do at work. Classically conditioned to repress emotions, parents may demand unquestioned obedience while failing to express their feelings in a healthy manner. Struggling to cope with their own emotions, these children do not learn the fundamental steps of dealing with conflict, which would benefit them throughout the school years, as well as when they enter the workforce.

As Vestal and Jones (2004) concluded, "conflict naturally occurs in human interaction and, if managed properly, can be a very constructive avenue for needed change. Unfortunately, conflict often causes emotional upset and challenges the communication capacity of most adults". Raised by overprotective or "helicopter" parents, these children may grow to lack:

- core social-emotional skills, which is developed through negotiating conflict.

- relationship problem-solving skills, a core characteristic of leadership.

- independency and self-help skills.

- awareness of people, as well as their environment.

- ambition and leadership skills coveted by organizations.

While every parent wants their children to grow up with more opportunities than they had, coping with a "professional" environment may prevent their children from learning the core skills necessary to succeed.

There's Hope in Confusion!

Welcome to big business, centuries in the making! Exploiting workers has a direct affect on producing quality workers in future generations, yet this injustice has been continuously cycled throughout history. Is it a stretch to believe that workers from centuries of old felt the same when faced with similar exploitation? Is this the future that is already set for our children? Although misconceptions have been reinforced for generations, there is hope! Working for a militant, top-down organization, there are many opportunities to create a more genial atmosphere, even for those not in management positions. Many stressful workdays are a result of an unstable environment; whether disagreements with management decisions, or ineffective communication between coworkers. Confusion and conflict create stress for all parties, however during these volatile times, opportunities for true leadership emerge.

The higher up an organization's hierarchy, the more often supervisors will encounter complex problems with no simple, straightforward answer. Because it's their responsibility, managers have no choice but to face these inevitable problems. Though, how your supervisor reacts during these times will show you their true leadership abilities, as well as give yourself an opportunity to gain affluence. During times of peril, Jentz and Murphy (2005) conclude that poor managers often:

- deny they are confused.

- hide their confusion for fear of losing respect.

- blame subordinates for circumstances.

- act in control while disregarding any constructive feedback.

- attempt a "quick fix" to restore confidence.

- show a take-charge attitude so not to show incompetence.

(These are most certainly characteristics of an "Ostrich" mentality)

Many times failure to recognize or embrace confusion results in poor decisions. This, in effect, undermines communication and creates distrust between employees and supervisors. Poor management practices also hurt the organization as whole by not taking advantage of critical learning opportunities. As distrust continues to build, supervisors are offered less information from employees, making it more difficult to make correct decisions, while also cultivating a reputation of indifference.

While times of uncertainty may seem overwhelming to the greatest of leaders, "in fact, confusion turns out to be a fruitful environment in which the best managers thrive by using the instability around them to open up better lines of communication, test their old assumptions and values against the changing realities, and develop more creative approaches to problem solving" (Jentz & Murphy, 2005). True leaders are able to use an unstable environment as a resource to promote new ideas and take advantage of learning opportunities, while also reinforcing authority over subordinates.

As the superintendent sat with her business manager, chief deputy, and senior aide, she sought to create an aggressive reform effort in a tight timeframe. Stating the problem as straightforward, the superintendent admitted to the time constraints, preventing them from speaking about the details, but she acknowledged her confidence in the team to construct a strong draft plan.

Viewing the time constraints as a significant problem and the course of action unclear, the deputy was confused about how to construct the draft plan. Not wanting to appear incompetent and lose the confidence of his subordinates, he decided to hide his confusion and take charge of the project.

Hashing out a work plan, the business manager was also unclear of the superintendent's expectations, but was relieved that he was not leading the project. Concealing his confusion, he also saw the deputy as confident, which eased his concerns, and he began helping to prepare the plan.

When the superintendent saw the draft plan was only 60% on target, she was caught off guard. Considering the problem, she was confused how her top staff failed to prepare a plan that should have been easy to create. Masking her confusion, she chided her staff for not focusing. Critical weeks and hundreds of staff hours were wasted.

In the aftermath, the superintendent admitted that she had concealed her confusion to the team and asked why they chose to do the same. Gradually, the chief deputy and the business manager admitted to their own facade, afraid of being seen as incompetent by the superintendent. (Jentz & Murphy, 2005)

Confusion and conflict provide opportunities for growth, and not just for supervisors. By following the suggested steps, every worker may use times of uncertainty to further their career aspirations.

Step 1: Embrace your confusion

While many people would rather hide their confusion, thereby frustrating supervisors when expectations are not met, the situation must be confronted. Asking questions shows a willingness to follow a superior's lead, while also gaining valuable information to complete a task properly.

Step 2: Assert your need to make sense

Admit your feelings to a supervisor with conviction, whether confusion of expectations or frustration at the problem. While not directing fault towards your supervisor (it is never wise to bite the hand that feeds you), admit the problem is causing troubled feelings and more explanation is necessary. By hiding your confusion and not completing tasks as expected, your supervisor may fulfill your fears and view you as incompetent and unwilling to communicate.

Step 3: Question proactively

By asking an insightful question, you may assert authority over fellow co-workers by creating an opportunity for them to join in your inquiry. Offer suggestions of necessary information so you may better complete a task and a supervisor may view you as a leader of your coworkers. Guiding interactions between managers and colleagues will result in greater affluence, while ultimately benefitting everyone involved.

Step 4: Listen reflectively and learn

"Reflective listening sounds simple but is actually an acquired skill that requires repeated practice... and even after you have learned how to do it, you will still encounter major challenges in applying it to real-world situations." (Jentz & Murphy, 2005) When reflective listening is completed properly, your coworkers will feel they have been heard and your supervisor will develop trust in you, leading to future collaboration during critical moments.

Social Problems

While confusion and conflict provide opportunities to improve communication and overall management skills, there are still many circumstances out of a worker's control. As business organizations compete with rivals, striving to maximize profit, eventually the economy peaks before bottoming out, resulting in a recession. Though the wealthy often retain their riches, it is the working class which receives much of the burden. Piecing together the economic shards, a new foreboding dawn arises for workers and their families.

As past generations of workers have already tempered expectations for their children, experiencing a recession is an especially ugly beast. An economic quake resulting in a scarcity of jobs, even for the most experienced of workers, sends an air of uncertainty wavering throughout the working class. Those at the peak of their careers are left to wonder if they would be back to work the next day. Through this downturn, workers seeking career advice begin to take heed to a new set of philosophies. Job security is non-existent when there is no guarantee of employment. Everyone is self-employed when considering your family a business. If a household's economy is unsustainable, as workers struggle to pay bills, an uncertain future for the next generation is also created.

While working parents are forced to consider emergency alternatives, the next generation is affected in a multitude of ways. Children, perceptive to their family's fears, reciprocally worry for their parents. Students from struggling families may be distracted at school, and as grades begin to slip, their future becomes as questionable as their parents. Some adolescents drop out of school altogether, sacrificing their future in order to help the immediate needs of their family. For similar reasons, students planning to obtain higher education must put their aspirations on hold, resulting in a less educated workforce.

As Jay MacLeod (2009) observed while interviewing a former student, "he left school with the understanding that he would be employed full-time, and he was mildly content with his situation: 'I gotta job. It ain't a good job, but other things will come along.' Two weeks later, he was laid off". Over the generations, an untold number of similar stories reinforce the idea that workers understand tremulous economic grounds and make decisions accordingly; even resorting to menial, low paying jobs with few benefits.

The next generation on the verge of entering the workforce, are often hesitant when asked about the future. This hesitancy, not from indecision but because of circumstance, is a result of the lack of choices when seeking working opportunities. Though difficult to ponder a bleak outlook, potential workers view planning for the future as futile. Like their parents, adolescents are already jaded, knowing their future is paved with hard, unrewarding work. "Perhaps at a younger age they had dreams for their futures. At ages sixteen, seventeen, and eighteen, however, their own job experiences as well as those of family members have contributed to a deeply entrenched cynicism about their futures" (MacLeod, 2009).

Preschool children have the understanding to question social imbalances such as race, gender, and economic status, yet the wisest of men have trouble answering. Why are some people rich and others poor? With the economy in a recession, people are looking for answers to challenging questions.

The Myth of Meritocracy

Jose Menendez was a perfectionist who, by his son's account could never do things too flawlessly. An impoverish immigrant, he had risen to become a millionaire in the entertainment industry, founding a video distribution business. Taking notice of his humble roots, a journalist once used his example as true testimony to the American Dream.

Coming from Cuba at age 15, he dedicated himself to success. Known as an extremely hard worker, and described as the brightest, hardworking businessman they had known, he dedicated every possible hour to getting ahead. Intensely aggressive and very competitive, he was equipped with all the necessary skills to succeed in the extravagant entertainment lifestyle of America.

As with many parents, Jose also had a strong desire to see his sons succeed. Teaching the same passion that made him a successful businessman, he drilled his sons in the sport of tennis, urging them to conquer their peers on and off the court. With their father's ambition, the older son would soon graduate from Princeton, the younger was accepted into UCLA. Teaching his boys, as he succeeded, to be ruthless against rivals, they also learned to do whatever it takes to get ahead.

In his $4 million estate, Jose spent the evening of August 20, 1989 in the den with his wife, eating fresh berries and cream. Likely more puzzled than frightened when Erik and Lyle burst into the room with shotguns, he and his wife were executed by the sons they raised with grand ambitions.

In the aftermath, the two sons, in their father's spirit, wasted no time putting their insurance claims to good use. Lyle, who dropped out of Princeton, used his share to buy a popular cafe and quickly made plans to start a chain of restaurants. Erik, with aspirations to play professional tennis, dropped out of college and hired a professional coach for $50,000 a year. While the brothers were eventually sentenced to life in prison, the police perceived the killings as financially influenced (Derber, 1996).

"As for many Americans, work is important not as an end in itself but as a means to an end – money" (MacLeod, 2009). While workers of all ages struggle in our economy, the simple truth is, everything revolves around $. Many people have aspirations to own a small business, whether a corner store or a pizza shop, yet reality attests that it takes $ to make $. Menial jobs usually require a diploma, license, or regulation requirement, and while coming out of the worker's pocket, employment is still not guaranteed even after obtaining the correct paperwork.

In fact, for the lower class, it actually costs $ to be broke. Banks, which charge for insufficient funds, are making a profit off people who cannot afford such fees. Flat-rate ticket violations also do not consider economic status, thereby creating harsher penalties for the lower class. Interest rates, dedicated to those who cannot afford $ up front, charge per payment, while people with wealth receive lower rates. All the while, those same banks warn consumers to save their $, by giving it to them. Conserving $ is a difficult task for workers struggling to pay bills in the here and now. It's also difficult to teach the next generation $ management skills when there isn't any $ to manage. Planning for the future and questioning the present are luxuries afforded to those with basic needs met.

The new "professional" ideology, which emphasizes perceptions, has cultivated the myth of meritocracy, which continues to stereotype the lower class. Jokes about homelessness and poverty abound in "family friendly" television, but when art and music is created out of social-economic anguish, it is attacked for allegedly being harmful to society. Multi-ethnic teenagers with tattoos, wearing dark, baggy clothes, often portrayed as the villain, have become America's new nightmare.

On October 23, 1989 in the city of Boston, Charles and Carol Stuart left a birthing class at a local hospital and walked to their nearby car. Within minutes, Charles received a gunshot wound to the abdomen while Carol, eight months pregnant, was killed.

Interviewed by police, Charles pointed the finger at a young, black hoodlum as the culprit. With images of gang-related, minority youths, America immediately felt for Charles and his lost wife and child. Collecting hundreds of thousands of dollars in insurance, he fulfilled his lifelong dream of opening a restaurant. Through such a tragedy, Charles created his own American Dream.

Two months later, America was stunned when police was alerted by his brother about Charles' involvement. A self-made hero, allured by the American Dream, Charles Stuart murdered his wife and child and spun a tale, instinctively believed by all of America. Taking advantage of a nation's deepest social anxieties, Americans were forced to question their own understanding of race and social classes (Derber, 1996).

Fueling the fire of stereotypes are television and movies which glorify rags to riches stories. While they promote a view of an open society, where hard work and moral values are rewarded, worker's own experiences, as well as those of their families, friends, and neighbors, contradict the myth of the American Dream. Questioning the very core of meritocracy, they see a variety of people, including those with marketable skills, struggle to gain employment. One is left to consider, if hard-working, dedicated people cannot find employment, what hope is there for them? As expectations are lowered, a lack of work experience and education results in the next generation being unable to develop the necessary skills when an opportunity does arise.

Mo' $, Mo' $

"During the 1990's, the rich got richer and the poor mostly stood still – CEO's pay increased by 571 percent, while hourly workers' take-home went up only 37 percent, barely beating inflation" (Bolman & Deal, 2003). Growing up witnessing these blatant financial imbalances, it's near impossible to convince the next generation that each person is helping to make a better society. Instead, the same historical perceptions of greedy businesses are reinforced once again. How is it possible for the next generation to contend in a social-economic game which is rigged from the start? Witnessing these injustices, the next generation has developed a new view of higher social classes.

- If I had their $ to start with, I'd make it rich too.

- A rich kid would have a better chance to get a job than me.

- You need to know people to succeed, and their parents have connections.

- I have to struggle more than they do, there's less hurdles in their path.

- They won't hire from our neighborhood because of its reputation.

(Here is where we begin to "run in circles" without a clear forward direction.)

While "a million and a half houses declare bankrupt every year" (Schor, 9), America's fixation with consuming materialistic items has become a billion dollar industry. As a result, the next generation has become a historically unprecedented target of commercialization. "Kids and teens are now the epicenter of American consumer culture. They command the attention, creativity, and dollars for advertisers. Their tastes drive marked trends. Their opinions shape brand strategies. Yet few adults recognize the magnitude of this shift and its consequences for the futures of our children and of our culture" (Schor, 2004)

Since they were in diapers, the next generation has been immersed in world of corporate logos, commercials, and websites. Even schools have become a new target of marketing, further creating a commercialized culture. In fact, many marketing campaigns exploit the anxieties of peer pressure and parental restraint, thereby creating conflict between children and parents. Those believing children are wholesome and innocent are naive to assume they are not also susceptible to greed and corruption. Says Mary Prescott, an advertising executive, "at the end of the day, my job is to get people to buy things... It's a horrible thing, and I know it" (Schor, 99).

Final Questions

One man, worth $100 billion on the stock market, had so much financial power, a colleague boasted, "I am the fella who determines what the changes will be. If I don't finance it, it ain't gonna happen. I get to decide who's going to get capital to make the future. Now, I ask you – what's more romantic than that?" (Derber, 1996). Ask any child about the stock market and they can tell you it's all about $. Though I must ask, what would society be like if $100 billion was invested in schools?

Public schools: America's social microcosm! Communities with financial capital are able to raise children who attend schools taught by experienced, knowledgeable teachers. Schools without such means suffer from the same social problems of violence, sex, and drugs as the neighborhoods they reside. How is it possible to obtain a truly just society when the public schools our children attend suffer from financial apartheid?

Aside from money, why do schools not teach social skills along with academic subjects? While learning about science and mathematics, children may be taught core social-emotional skills through relationship problem-solving, negotiating conflicts, and embracing confusing situations. In an optimal learning environment, where children are given autonomy and are able to express themselves freely, they will learn to thrive instead of how to survive. The same human resource philosophies exemplified by Robert Owen and Elton Mayo, when applied to businesses, schools, or any administration organization, creates an idealistic environment where each individual can flourish.

A Summary

Throughout history, the common perception of workers has been to work hard and do what they're told. Pioneers of human resource philosophies, such as Robert Owens, proved that treating workers admirably results in increased profits. However, adding to the historical perception of businesses sacrificing people for profits, "even as these research results pile up, trends in actual management practice are, in many instances, moving in a direction exactly opposite to what this growing body of evidence prescribes" (Bolman & Deal, 135).

Whether kings or CEOs, for profit or quality of life, the goals of a governing administration reverberates throughout an organization's hierarchy, and seeps into the worker's home. Although all monetarily run organizations must be aware of finances, businesses solely on a quest for profit often produce frustrated workers, while those focused on the well-being of its employees cultivate a positive, efficient working environment. While workers give their time, energy, talent, and ideas in return for $ to support families, their children are intuitive of their attitudes of employment.

The next generation, receiving tempered expectations from their parents, must face a new challenge of "professional" ideologies. Working in environments where conflict is avoided and emotions are suppressed, these philosophies also reverberate in the household, resulting in children with a lack of social-emotional skills. Unable to develop these aptitudes through negotiating conflict, these children are less prepared to succeed in top-down administrations, such as schools and, eventually, the workforce.

As workers and their families cope with detrimental working environments, there is hope during confusing, unstable circumstances. By confronting confusion, workers and supervisors alike have an opportunity to improve communication and practice creative problem-solving skills. Unfortunately while poor managers often hide or deny their confusion, embracing volatile situations through questioning and reflective listening, will benefit all parties involved, as well as further a worker's career aspirations.

At work, employees may be able to influence change; however social problems, such as a recession, are out of their control. As the economy bottoms out, jobs become scarce and new philosophies emerge in the working class. Fears of job security and household income directly affect a worker's mentality, which is passed to the next generation. Adolescents feeling obligated to postpone higher education, or drop out of school altogether, in order to help the immediate needs of their family, result in a less educated, less experienced workforce.

Although their future appears bleak, the next generation shows an understanding of these social imbalances, and is questioning the very core of meritocracy. Given no reasonable explanation of why people are rich or poor, they watch as the media promotes an open society, where hard work and moral values are rewarded, yet their own families struggle to find employment. Worse, they see themselves being stereotyped, which they believe affects their ability to find consistent employment.

Raised with commercialization and perceiving a materialistic society as a result, the next generation shudders as the rich continue to get richer. Being historically unprecedented targets of commercialization, marketing strategies exploiting fears of peer pressure and parental authority have created a divide between children and their parents. Unaware that children are susceptible to such influences, adults don't realize this dangerous shift in culture, or the consequences it may have on society.

While workers, families, and children look for answers to complex social questions, the schools they've all attended are a microcosm of the problem. As stock market businessmen delegate billions of dollars, schools continue to be a victim of apartheid, making it impossible to attain a truly just society. If children were taught core social-emotional skills in schools, idolizing the very human resource philosophies exemplified by Robert Owen, they would learn to thrive exactly like workers treated admirably.

So, What's the Answer?

As businesses continue to grow, knowledgeable employees become more valuable. New workers cost time and money by not understanding the products and services they offer, thereby making poor quality products and giving poor service. Aside from salaries, they also expense valuable resources to adequately train, yet may still make costly mistakes learning the job. Properly compensating a knowledgeable, experienced worker becomes more justifiable than paying to train a new employee.

Organizations which try to incorporate a human resource philosophy, but fear workers will abuse the system, often fail before they start. Sending mixed signals, such as "you make the decision, so long as it's what I want" and "do what you think is right, but make sure I agree", elude the core of the human resource approach. Many traditional managers are unsuccessful because:

- they fear losing control and/or spoiling workers.

- investing in people is a long-term process.

- evaluation is based on short-term, immediate results.

- financial statistics are more easily understood than complex human issues (Bolman & Deal, 2003).

To incorporate a successful philosophy, an organization needs to fully commit to human resource strategies. Halfhearted attempts to treat people admirably will result in expected failure. "To succeed, managers must learn to embrace a new approach – one that is deceptively easy to describe but remarkably hard to practice" (Jentz & Murphy, 2005).

In 1985, a joint venture between American and Japanese car manufacturers sought to reopen a plant in Fremont, California. Choosing a workforce from 5,000 employees laid off the year before, many workers had a rebellious reputation during their previous time. Within two years, worker absenteeism was down 18%, and the plant was producing higher quality cars with lower labor costs than any other site in the company.

During the joint venture, the American manufacturer provided the plant and workers, while Japanese manufacturers supplied the car and production processes, as well as managed the plant. Through a human resource philosophy, workers and managers wore the same uniforms, parked in the same lots, and used the same cafeteria. Designing small, self-managing groups, employees created their own jobs and worked each task in rotation. The plant motto was "there are no managers, no supervisors, only team members". (Bolman & Deal, 2003)

When workers had a grievance, a union representative and a human resource staff member would meet immediately to work out the problem. If the assembly line's pace was too great, workers could pull a cord to stop the belt and help would arrive shortly. While management initially feared the cord would be abused by tired workers, they were pleasantly surprised when it was a complete success.

The American manufacturer was so pleased with the results of this newly renovated plant that they decided to base the entire corporation on a human resource philosophy. Eventually becoming a fad, the idea was introduced weakly, which resulted in expected failure. When asked why the human resource philosophy did not take hold in the American manufacturer, the Japanese plant president said he was afraid "upper management does not understand the basic concept". (Bolman & Deal, 2003)

"We often forget how much we rely on our world to make sense until our world is turned upside down by new information or changing circumstances." (Jentz & Murphy, 2005) Organizations which successfully incorporate a human resource philosophy are rewarded in a variety of ways. By fulfilling the needs of employees, these organizations attract motivated, dedicated workers, and are able to be selective when acquiring new talent. Because skilled, experienced workers provide an organization with higher production, better costumer service, and innovative ideas, investing in personnel yields a competitive edge against rival businesses. Less likely to make costly mistakes, loyal employees will continue to grow and develop within the organization, instead of looking for better opportunities (Bolman & Deal, 2003).

While businesses may be able to incorporate some these ideas, truly successful organizations are able to change the entire structure of their hierarchy to incorporate a human resource philosophy. Traditional businesses inherently keep information confidential; however progressive organizations specialize in developing transparency between workers and management. Two-way communication builds trust, while managers are also able to utilize valuable ideas from workers. In businesses of old, it is easy to decipher the economic class of employees by observing office size and access to perks; however new age organizations promote egalitarianism by reducing social status symbols, while incorporating signs of equality and togetherness.

Progressive organizations also create transparency by enacting an open-book management philosophy. With no a better way to show trust, employees who learn the business side of their job are also more apt to contribute to the company. By understanding how their contribution directly affects the business, employees are more willing to complete tasks productively. Organizations have also experimented with new pay systems, with much success. Paid a starting rate, employees are able to learn new jobs, and consequently receive more pay, while negating any competitive nature between coworkers. Without a need for employees to hold onto skills or information to protect job status, the organization creates a more knowledgeable, intrinsically-driven workforce. (Bolman & Deal, 2003)

Ricardo Semler, taking over his father's Brazilian manufacturing company, installed a new philosophy of management. Using an unorthodox approach, workers hired new employees, evaluated supervisors, and voted on the company's major decisions, resulting in extraordinary productivity. At one time, the employees outvoted Semler, preventing him from acquiring a new plant he wanted to purchase. Another time, workers voted to purchase an abandoned factory Semler didn't want. Making it an incredible success,

Semler saw no need for the business to grow, yet it grows anyway because innovative employees continue to invent new businesses (Bolman & Deal, 2003).

> *"The key to management is to get rid of all the managers. The key to getting work done on time is to stop wearing a watch. The best way to invest corporate profits is to give them to the employees. The purpose of work is not to make $. The purpose of work is to make the employees, whether working stiffs or top executives, feel good about life."*
>
> - Edmund Burke

To the Next Generation

At the turn of the century, the Wright Brothers experimented with gliders for the first time in aviation history. On July 21, 1969, Neil Armstrong was the first person to ever step on the moon. In 70 years, technology has taken us from Kitty Hawk to the Moon. Yet, 200 years of business research has only begun to realize the enormous potential of people, aviation as an example. What could we accomplish in the next century if we focus on human resource strategies and teach them to the next generation?

To the next generation: when you are promoted to positions of superiority or begin your own administration organizations, remember this: Treat your team admirably! Not only does it prove to increase profits, it is helping to reverse the cycle of poverty! And never forget, continue to teach the next next generation, because they will continue the mission. Always focus on the next generation and humanity will prevail!

Works Cited

Bolman, Lee G. & Deal, Terrence E. (2003). Reframing Organizations: Artistry, Choice, and Leadership. Jossey-Bass.

Buckley, M. (2000). Cognitive-Developmental Considerations in Violence Prevention and Intervention. Professional School Counseling.

Derber, Charles. (1996). The Wilding of America: How Greed and Violence are Eroding Our Nation's Character. St. Martin's Press, Inc.

Jentz, Barry C. & Murphy, Jerome T. (Jan. 2005). "Embracing Confusion: What Leaders Do When They Don't Know What to Do." Phi Delta Kappan.

Macleod, Jay. (2009). Ain't No Makin' It: Aspirations and Attainment in a Low-Income Neighborhood. Westview Press.

O'Toole, James (1995). Leading Change: Overcoming the Ideology of Comfort and the Tyranny of Custom. Jossey-Bass.

Schor, Juliet B. (2004). Born to Buy: The Commercialized Child and The New Consumer Culture. Scribner.

Trahair, R.C.S. (2001). "George Elton Mayo." Thoemmes.

Vestal, Anita & Jones, Nancy A. (2004). Peace Building and Conflict Resolution in Preschool Children.

Principle Four

Distant Teams and Clients are not happy! Kevin Brooks will be writing the following section about this key principle.

You would know instantly if you happened onto a distance sales call with Kevin Brooks. You will feel this conversation. I know that is the response I had to our initial phone call to discuss a mutual product. Half the way through the call, I forgot why I had called. I was caught up in the personal stories that he shared and pleasantly turned back to me to show how they related. I was sold. Then, I wanted to meet this amazingly smooth phone salesperson.

I visited Kevin on site of his sales director position. I saw the same smoothness with his team members that I experienced on the call.

As I interviewed Kevin, I asked if he used a script at his call centers. He told me absolutely. Then, I asked how I wasn't able to detect it as a consumer.

He quickly schooled me on the purpose of a script to keep details organized and covered, but never to think for one second that any two people were alike.

I have learned more about distant sales and distant team leadership from Kevin within the last two years than in years of reading books on the topic.

As call centers and distant team leadership are on the rise, Kevin's work in Principle 4 is critical to getting all generations to work together effectively. The following essay is written entirely by Kevin Brooks, and is included here by permission of the author.

Growing and managing teams that are in multiple locations is a special challenge to generational leadership. There is a contradiction at play. The more seasoned team members are traditionalists and baby boomers and the top portion of generation X. They seem to like to be on-site with the core of the company and not isolated in a field office or at home. Yet, they are the team members that are known to be more disciplined and compliant to parameters that hold distant teams together. The latter part of generation X, generation flux and the Millennials seem to prefer the flexibility of independent work. Yet, they are the ones that are hard to locate and corral even if they do work right down the hall from you.

In this section, we are going to look at managing a team long-distance and also at offering great customer service to clients and customers that we cannot see face-to-face. Both require communication skills that go beyond the standard. Both are being taxed with impatient callers and frustrated with multiple interpretations of instructions and services expectations. Both are causing a growing tension.

Distant Teams

First, we are going to look at teams. There are at least 15 communication channels available to us today. Some cannot be used with distance teams like face-to-face and bulletin boards. That causes us to look to other channels. If we still want to see someone as we speak with them, we do have Skype, Facetime, and other screen-share services. Those are good if both sides know how to use them and both are can commit to a meeting time. If there is the added challenge of multiple time zones and access to service areas, then we have to consider communication that goes through words and tone only. That is a huge challenge.

Experts in Communication share that 55% of our message is sent through our body language. They say that 38% goes through tone, and 7% is contained within the words. Channels that lack the visual component are trying to maximize a message while lacking 55% of the power. We can still be effective. Most people don't properly use the power of body language when they have it available anyway. We will hone in on perfecting the tone and the word choice.

Since tone is 38%, let's address that. Tone in a voice can carry anger, disinterest, arrogance, fear, doubt, confusion, happiness, excitement, sarcasm, and probably others. This is going to be a battle of mind over matter. To cover tone is pretty much impossible. It is best to get your mind into the right place before you pick up the phone or recording device that is going to carry your message.

Emotion in the workplace is rarely good when it is in the anger range. Anger destroys careers and relationships. Frustration should be as far as we allow ourselves to go. To do that, we need to go logical once we hit frustration. I do this by collecting data and taking notes. If you are writing as quickly as someone is speaking, you will be struggling to keep up and cannot connect emotion to their words. After I collect the data and take the notes, I step away to adjust my emotions. I can do that either by taking a break from the office or person. If that is not possible, I take the break mentally. I know that doing Math and problem-solving will require logic. I do those. I keep math books near my desks and keep problem-solving sites on my quick-keys. After attacking puzzles and math challenges, I can feel the tension levels coming down. I return to the thing or person that was causing my initial frustration after I feel myself in logic mode. That is where problems get solved.

I travel on many planes with my job. At the end of a long work day, the last thing I want to do is sit beside someone who is agitated with their job or the world in general and wants to "share". If I have a choice of seats, I purposely seek out the Sudoku puzzle books. They aren't angry. They are in logic mode. They are going to be pleasant and unemotional. Perfect for the frequent flyer! Of course, I will sit beside them and start with, "so, where you from?" I'm teasing. This is a golden moment, I am going to respect their space. It was on a plane though that I noticed something in the eyes of someone in logic mode that is asked to flip back to emotional. I had to interrupt someone doing a puzzle to let them know that the flight attendant wanted them to move their bag. I was offering to put it under my seat for them. The person stared blankly at me for a second or two before reconnecting to me. Then, they could hear me and respond. During those two seconds, I could see their eyes shift from left to right. They came out of logical into emotional.

The same thing happens in reverse if we need to shift from emotional into logical. The eyes will shift in the other direction. I don't not think that you will care to go to a mirror to watch this. After all, you are emotional when this process begins. You might prefer to squeeze a stress ball or do some push-ups. If the stress levels are high in emotion, you might prefer to take a walk around the building, or the city. Whatever works for you. But, I thought you might like to know you're your eyes are shifting.

Sometimes, our tones cannot be adjusted with only going logical. This happens when logic supports your emotion. You know that you are right and have the data to prove it. This could still damage the communication. It is best to have yourself out of overwhelm as well and be prepared to lay out your communication with clarity.

I have learned this trick from being a parent. My first born would go into a store with $20.00 of birthday money and spend hours trying to decide what to buy. I don't remember what I did back then to get him to a conclusion, but I do remember being very frustrated with the time spent there. These days, I watch other parents facing the same challenge in toy stores. As their child escalates to tears and raised voice, I stroll by and drop the one line that used to drive me crazy when I was trying to get my first born under control, "mine are grown". I'm teasing. I want to, but the glazed, crazy look in their eyes tell me that this might not be the time to taunt them. I am just happy to know that I no longer go through this process. I have learned how to switch my children from emotional to logical. It works with subordinates, co-workers, and friends as well.

I tell my children to gather the things that they like that will meet the spending limit and bring them to me. We lay them side-by-side. Just for fun, I still ask them which one they want, and I get the same answer that I did with my first-born. "I want them all". Then, I simply nudge them by asking which one they will chose to put back first. They make that decision in less than 5 seconds. After I do that, my job is done. I have put them into logical mode. They will finish the game. They systematically eliminate items until they are down to the one that they probably wanted all along.

Before you get onto the call or start a recording, make sure that you have cleared frustration and overwhelm. Have a systematic plan or outline of your ideas. Know your limits and be prepared for the negotiation. There are many great programs on negotiation available on line and in books to help you with that part.

Now, you are ready to choose your words. When I was studying speech-writing in college, our professor gave us one of the most interesting assignments. He asked us to write a speech that was worthy to be delivered by a presidential candidate. I went to the library thinking that this would be easy. After all, I had been studying journalism for awhile and knew my position on the topic he assigned us.

I sat in the library for hours. I realized that I could not start to write the words until I had clarity on several things. I had to consider the candidate's image. Was he one that liked to call the shots with authority or one that liked to come across as a motivator. Was he going to use this opportunity to shift his image in any manner, or was he happy with the path and polling numbers that he was seeing. Then, I had to consider the power of the feeling words. Did he "disagree" with this, "dislike" this, "despise" this, or "feel repulsed" by this.

Then, I got stuck for an entire day on three words. They are I, You, and We. You is a word that attacks. It also gets attention. It is like taking the first shot. Do you want to? For the most part, you is dangerous word. Your opponent will put up their defense system and will most likely shoot back. If you want to test it, go home tonight and start your conversation with the word "you". Not as in, "you are wonderful" or "you are handsome"; rather in "you forgot…" or "you never...", or "you always…" Yea, good luck with that. The defense systems will probably go up and you are looking at a re-turned shot. This could go on for hours until someone puts up the white flag. That someone will probably be use since "you started it".

You is not always the wrong choice. In sales, for example, we know that you can't get a sale until you engage the opponent. The best salespersons know how long to attack with "you" before reading the frustration level on the other side to know to switch to the understanding "I" language. "You" is also effective for supervisors to lead an employee to raise their level of performance. Starting with, "John you know this isn't your best work", "you are capable of more", "what is happening with you?" will bring a strong response. John will indeed go on the defensive, but that is exactly what you were looking for. In his defense, you can find what is bothering him.

I is usually the better choice. It keeps defense systems down. "I've noticed…", I'm feeling.." "I am wondering…" The danger with I can be when it comes across as arrogant. I can establish credibility, but it can also sound self-promotion.

"We" is a unifying word if you are 100% sure that the people you are speaking for actually agree with your statement. As I was writing this mock-up speech for a presidential candidate, I realized how powerful the word "you" can be. And, how maddening it was if someone spoke for you and they did not have your buy-in.

We may not be running for political office, but we would be wise to go through all of the same steps. When communicating as a leader, know your image, know when you want to move that image, think through your words of emotion, and deliver them thoughtfully. They stick.

If you are managing a distance team, the phone and recording etiquette rules are critical. One of the great tools available today allow for a daily touch in with a distance team is voice memos. They are available as an App and on other phones. They work well with distance teams by giving you an advantage in several ways:

- You can choose the time to make and send the voice memo (you aren't restricted by a clock)

- You can keep a permanent record of what you said

- You can replay and re-record it until it sounds the way you want it to and you are sure that you have not mis-spoken.

- You can send it to multiple people at the same time through their email systems

- You can know when they opened the email

- You can know who has the information before you proceed with a decision

- You will most likely receive a response from them through their email which gives you a permanent record of what they said in response.

- You can record them when your tone is positive and you are emotions are in check

Distant Clients

We might as well dive into the negative feedback we get from distant clients. These are the things that they bother them when we deal with them on the telephone.

- We are working from a script

- The person answering doesn't have the answers

- We transfer them several times

- The call gets dropped, and they are not called back

- Language and accent barriers

- Excessive wait times

- Departments don't communicate their information

- Deceit of our location (making is sound local when it is not)

- Requiring them to repeat information

Building on the word and tone choice from the beginning of this chapter, we should work to eliminate every one of these bullet points. It is all in the training and treatment of the people answering the phones.

There are times that I have dealt with an apathetic call receiver. I have called back to announce that I was hung up on by so-and-so and I want a supervisor to pull the recording of the call that I told was being made so that we could go through and I could be vindicated. What do you think I was told? You got it, "We don't really make those recordings." Are you kidding me? You mean I have been polite to unpleasant call center employees for all these years in hopes that I would be perceived as the reasonable one only to find out that it was just a façade? I felt shorted. People on the telephone are just as important as those standing before you.

Ostriches is going to support the team member that is trying to stay positive and speak with clarity when they are dealing with less-than-reasonable callers. It also supports the company that is guiding them.

When we look at training team members that are going to be representing us on the telephone, it is important to revisit the basics of phone etiquette.

- Speak with clarity and directly into the receiver

- Announce and introduce anyone on the call

- Inform the caller if they are being recorded (and be honest)

- Inform the caller of your location

- Inform the caller of your name and your title

- Get the caller's phone number first incase the call is dropped

- If the call must be passed onto someone else, remain on the line until the other person has connected and received the call. Share with the person you are passing the call to all of the information that you have collected from the caller. Don't make them repeat themselves

- Don't jump to conclusions or judge, stay open to receive

- Be a patient listener

- Don't apologize for your company. Show empathy with other word choices. Apologies can create emotion and assume liability

- Don't speak from a script. The caller can sense that. Use bullet points and check-off sheets if you must.

- Try to own the problem

Using the "I" language discussed in the first part of this chapter is critical. Most mistakes are made by people using "you" language. The other person on the call will most likely get defensive and the battle will ensue. Without the advantage of body language, people on phone are much harder to get back into control. It is nearly impossible to calm them and retain their respect. It is important to get it right up front.

Though it is difficult to not take "you" language personally, a professional person will know that the best tactic is to keep using "I" language back until the person on the other side defuses and calms. I call this the "huff". They will eventually realize that they are not agitating you and they will use a heavy sign to retain control, but to de-escalate as well. This is where you win.

Listening skills are the most important part of connecting with a client on the phone. It is never wise to assume you know where they are going. Never finish their sentences. Take notes to slow yourself down and re-check your perception before answering.

We often hear that in order to be a great salesperson, you must have the gift of gab or be a great talker. We think this is true on the phone. Nothing could be further from the truth. People are not going to be impressed with a smooth talker, especially the younger generations. People do not care how much you know until they know how much you care. They can also sense if you are listening by the questions that you ask in return. Quoting back to them what you think you heard for their validation is a great way to show that you are really listening.

Interruptions are another thing that gets us in trouble with a caller. Interruptions can be as subtle as a sigh or an "un-huh" uttered every other sentence.

We don't want to go onto auto-pilot. That happens often with scripting. We will go much further by convincing someone that we are interested in them rather than trying to get them to hear us. One of the best ways to stay off a scripting path is to open with an engaging question. Asking if they are starting a great week? If they enjoyed their weekend? Then, allow time to really listen to their answers and start a mini-conversation.

Try to match their pace. If someone is a fast talker, try to step up to their pace. This might not be easy if you are also trying to be clear. A general rule though is that someone who speaks rapidly is also impatient, focused, and decisive. This wouldn't be the right person to ramble with. On the other hand, if they speak slowly, slow your pace as well adjust your energy level to their's. Slower speakers are often analytical or very sensitive. You wouldn't want to run over them on a call. Principle 5 will discuss more about behavorial styles.

Our studies show that on a telephone you might only have ten seconds to set the relationship. Use those seconds wisely. The best way to do that is to jump-start the positivity with an opening comment that assures them that you are going to be an attentive listener.

Call Centers

This last part of the chapter is to for call centers and those that perform collections or take calls from disgruntled customers.

Your job is tough! Let me validate you again. Your job is tough! It takes a very special person to come in every day in a positive mood only to sit down and start taking negative calls. The mind and emotional control that you exhibit is extraordinary.

The only way to win here is through a combination of not taking calls personally (that can't be), and convincing yourself that every call can be "won". It is a mistake to think that there isn't a solution. Most of us learn that when we become parents. You can't fire your kids. You have to look harder for the motivators, the hidden agendas, the secret desires, and the unspoken message. If you can do this on a telephone without having the advantage of body language, you are a master communicator. Most of your answers come from well-worded questions followed by silence.

One of the most affective questions that we find in getting people to open up and speak is using the word "surprise". "Surprise" does not lead the answer. It leaves things wise open.

An example would be, "Mrs. Johnson, now that you have been a client of ours for a few months, I am curious as to what has surprised you about our service to you?" Now, she is free to go positive or negative. She will most likely go directly to her honest answer.

We want to encourage those of you that do collections. Remember that the receiver is already on the defensive when you call. Treat them with respect even when they do not return it. Remember that you are helping them to build a solid financial future by getting their promised payments in on time. In many cases, you may be their last chance at building a financial future. They are probably missing other obligations as well. People who are pressured by debt are likely to be loyal to someone that treats them with respect and that they genuinely like. Since their credit may be bad, they aren't choosing who to pay by power. They are choosing their basic needs and those that make them feel good about themselves.

In the end, you may be the one person that boosts their self-esteem and helps them to get back on their feet.

PRINCIPLE FIVE

C ommunication has gone strategic! John Meluso will be writing the following section about this innovative principle.

John Meluso, CSP, has authored many great books in a career devoted to helping others to become their greatest. His work on bridging communication through reading the distinct markings in the iris of our eyes is a dead-on compliment to Herding Ostriches.

Generation X and Millennials want quick answers to questions that are proven. EyeTalk gives us that. John's work causes my seminar attendees to pause each day for questions. There is no dropping of the material and moving on. Break times usually find them huddled in circles going through the eye charts and using the light scope to read each others receiving/learning style.

EyeTalk makes the science easy. The ability to know your bosses', clients, subordinates and co-worker's preferred and effective communication style is a huge advantage. Whether the reader has goals of prosperity, winning, or simply keeping peace at the workplace, this is the information they need.

John is a Baby Boomer with a Flux mentality. He wants his cutting-edge work to be embraced by all of the generations in order to achieve the universal harmony we say we need to succeed.

John's work as presented in Herding Ostriches is about to go global. He has the app in development that could theoretically allow us know in an instance the receiving style in front of us through a simple photo taken with a cell phone.

Mostly, John Meluso is a part of this project because we share a point of view that the younger generations are not worse communicators than their older counterparts. We see them as more effective communicators that are capable of juggling many "conversations" at once. They wisely use technology to help them to streamline and record their conversations. We don't seem them as the demise of communication, but rather as the new and improved model.

The text in the following Principle is entirely written by John Meluso, and is printed here by permission.

Communication is the source of nearly every logistical and performance problem within a company.

As complicated as it is at this point, it is about to get worse. Principle 1 was dedicated to showing how the work environment is changing dramatically due to the mixture of generations. The ideology differences of the generations are impacting the approach to problem-solving. Generation Flux is embracing the study of "strategic communication". They are buying into the theory that there is a science to communication. They are digging deep for the answers to give them the edge.

By the time the Gen Nexters join the corporate mixture in four short years, communication is probably going to look something like the Tower of Babble. It's not too far from that right now. Some of the accusations heard often are:

- Fluxers only want to communicate through high-tech tools to confuse others

- Millennials have lost all social skills, as well as manners

- Generation X left face-to-face communications for buttons and have detached

- Baby Boomers won't embrace technology and are holding the rest of us back

- Traditionalists are clueless that a communication break-down even exists

These accusations are usually followed by finger pointing and apathy.

I was having dinner with a Baby Boomer business colleague recently and he directed my attention to a group of young adults sitting at a table behind us. He was sure that what we were witnessing was the problem with today's society. The four were sitting together, but rarely speaking. They were each on their cell phones, apparently texting someone else. He went on to tell me that what we were witnessing there would assuredly be the demise of the American culture.

As I had heard this statement many times in the past from other Baby Boomers, I knew what I had to do to cause him to re-think his prediction. I scanned the restaurant and found a table of Baby Boomers. I directed his attention to them. All four were sitting together, but rarely speaking. They were each hidden behind their individual copies of the Wall Street Journal. Then, I showed him the location of the Xers. They were at the bar facing ahead, rarely speaking. They were watching not one, but four, sports events on separate TV monitors. He smiled when I observed that at least the Millennials were communicating with someone, even if it was with texting.

Pointing fingers or playing the blame game gets us nowhere. Neither does making light of communication tools that others chose to use. The way to succeed at this game is to know how to utilize each of the communication tools and to know which one of them, when engaged, will give us the greatest chance of success.

There are at least fifteen channels of communication in the average business office. Most of us tend to rely on the one with which we are most comfortable. Sometimes, we just go with the channel that we think will save us time.

Email is our problem child. We chose email thinking that it will save us time and often find that it actually costs us more time as we later seek to clarify the meaning of our message. Email is an effective tool if it is properly utilized, but often we forget that it is a tool of logic, and not one of emotion. Tone cannot be detected in an email. Whatever we may think about the possibility to detect sarcasm, teasing, humor, urgency, and anger in emails, the language is not universal.

The definition of communication has always been the effective transfer of meaning and intention to bring about an intended result. To achieve an intended result, we have to first take responsibility for the communication we are about to send. Meaning, if we are the sender, we cannot blame the receiver if something goes awry.

This is the point where Fluxers and Millennials are leading the way. They have demonstrated a willingness to take responsibility. They have shown a willingness to study the art of communication. While many companies have embraced Behavioral Styles as a critical component of communication success, they have yet to embrace the impact of receiving styles. Fluxers and Millennials want to understand and use everything possible to succeed. As one wise Fluxer observed in a communication seminar, "Every attempt at communication is a negotiation, and winning a negotiation requires knowing everything I can about my receiver".

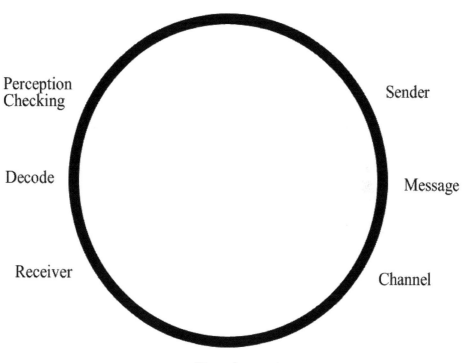

Communication Circle

We see the sender as the starting point followed by the message we are about to send. Before we examine the choice of channel, let's look at the encoding process. There are many factors to be considered in the encoding process that are not mentioned in the circle. Some might be cultural differences, rank of receiver vs. the rank of the sender, gender variances, state of mind of the receiver, the urgency of the message, legal considerations, the relationship between the sender and the receiver, etc. Those factors are often decided by a company's culture and therefore, not addressed here. We are going to take a look at the two mentioned, namely Behavioral Styles and Receiving Styles.

Great philosophers throughout history have theorized about the differences in people and ultimately generated what we know today as Behavioral Styles. Their goal has been a noble one: to help people understand themselves and each other so people might work in vocations that match their personality types and work more effectively with those around them. Achieving this would make people happier and create a more creative, productive and peaceful world to live in.

In ancient Greece, Hippocrates developed the concept of four temperaments — Melancholy, Sanguine, Phlegmatic, and Choleric. In 1923, Dr. Carl Jung wrote his definitive work, "Psychological Types," in which he describes four behavioral types: Intuiter, Thinker, Feeler, and Sensor. Social anthropologists tell us that there is evidence of these four behavioral types in cultures throughout the world.

Jung claimed he arrived at his system "through the study of all sorts of human types,1" and that his four orientations covered all humankind.

I came to the conclusion that there must be as many different ways of viewing the world [as there are psychological types]. The aspect of the world is not one, it is many—at least 16, and you can just as well say 360. You can increase the number of principles, but I found the most simple way is the way I told you . From Interview with Carl Jung by Richard Evans, University of Houston, in Zurich in 1957

Hippocrates and Carl Jung, and all the philosophers and scientists in between, understood that differences existed. The challenge was in how to describe and sort out these various types. More importantly: how do we apply this knowledge? Jung's main concern was not with theories in science or philosophy of science. It was with the fear of stereotyping. A psychological type, he said, is "just a skeleton to which you have to add the flesh... It is a means to an end. It only makes sense, such a scheme [of types] when you deal with practical cases." Acknowledging Dr. Jung's work and mirroring his concern for application in various profiles, other psychologists developed other versions of the personality profile. In 1926, American psychologist William Moulton Marston published "The Emotions of Normal People," which included a brief description of a system measuring Dominance, Influence, Steadiness and Compliance (DISC). Since then we've seen profiles by Myers-Briggs, Proformax, Dr. Tony Alessandra, and the new Australian model known as the Harrison Inner View. All these described models determine their specific categories with objective evaluations and interpretations of a self-administered test. All of these models are valuable, and are not mutually exclusive.

Using several profiles can help you be extremely accurate and measure different aspects of the human condition. The Myers-BriggsTM instrument is one of the most widely used personality inventories. Approximately 2,000,000 people a year take the MBTI® to improve work and personal relationships, increase productivity, and identify leadership and interpersonal communication preferences The MBTI® is a self-reporting questionnaire designed to make Jung's theory of psychological types understandable and useful in everyday life.

In business, managers use these tools to decide whom to hire. They also use them as a productivity tool for helping people to better understand themselves and their coworkers. These tools have supported individuals with self-understanding and development, career development and exploration, organizational development, team building, management and leadership training, problem solving, relationship counseling, education and curriculum development, academic counseling, and diversity and multicultural training. All of these personality instruments identify valuable differences among normal, healthy people – differences that can be the source of much misunderstanding and miscommunication.

The challenge associated with self-administered tests lies within the construct framework of the test. The Myers-Briggs administrators admit that they only give the test in English and that the test is best administered to people over the age of 14.

Do these facts limit the scope of the test? If an employee or new hire felt that certain answers might support their job procurement or advancement, might their answers shift? In the American culture, might the traditional role of male and female affect answers, with the test taker being concerned with how they appear to others based upon cultural norms? Might the way a child was reared affect their natural tendency for behaviors? Might a parent influence a child when the parent implies that a behavior is proper? Might a severe crisis distort, disorient, and substantially shift natural preferences? Now, what if these weren't factors at all in assessing style? Might there be something that would separate natural tendencies from learned or self-imagined preferences? Could there be a system that allowed accurate perception of a person's learning style at an early age and in any language so others could earlier and more effectively communicate with them in their style preference? Since human preferences are natural, could we determine types earlier through observation of some sort and be more objective in our determination? What about combining both Behavior Styles, testing, determining "What someone thinks they are!" with what they really are! Does who you THINK you are match who you REALLY are? Is there a definite way to determine WHO YOU REALLY ARE? The answer is yes, with eyeTalk.

We perceive the world through vision, hearing, touch, smell and taste, and communicate in all those senses. Communication occurs in an infinite variety of expressions in all those sensory channels.

The technology of instant communication all over the world — social media, telephone, radio, television, newspapers, magazines, movies, Express Mail, Priority Mail, bulk mail, Overnight Federal Express Mail, fax, e-mail, and libraries of centuries at the touch of a finger on the internet — inundates us with information and the opportunity to communicate. With this infinite amount of information from the largest variety of communication sources ever available, miscommunication is at a record high. It turns out that having more channels through which to communicate has not improved our situation.

We begin to change our relationships by changing our communication and interaction styles. With the infinite variety of ways to communicate, we must truly begin to understand our "best style," or our "preferred style" of interaction and communication. We must also begin to understand the styles of others, so we can consciously and efficiently communicate with those around us.

Our first efforts of communicating beyond Planet Earth were radio waves to the cosmos in all of Earth's known languages. Did we ask, "How do you communicate?" Did we care? We just expected "them" to respond to us.

Unfortunately, many of us have unconsciously been duplicating this egocentric communication pattern for too long. This style of communication shows no concern for those we are speaking to. In the early 1950s when Americans began to travel to Europe more frequently, we quickly garnered the label of "Ugly Americans" after the title of William Lederer's novel. This label actually spoke less to our physical appearance than our linguistic style. These "Ugly Americans" would travel around the world and expect every other culture to speak English and to have menus in English. Many Americans were disappointed when foreign food or customs did not match their American tastes and habits. Rather than adapting to the foreign county, they complained.

It's time (way past time, actually) to change that attitude. To change the attitude of "us versus them," we must appreciate each other's values and seek to learn from each other. Learning the 'what' of someone's behavior, and also when and how to use their specific behavior in our own lives, could only improve our relationship and also make our own lives easier.

Does using an emotional, sensitive behavior when balancing my checkbook make any sense when it means spending several hours trying to find a one-cent difference? Is that efficient or cost effective? Would a logical, analytical style be more valuable?

Does an analytical, logical style have any place in the whirlwind of love and romance? Being swept away is an integral aspect of being in love. Does a emotional whirlwind of passion and excitement contribute to making a sale or sustain a project through adversity? I know many people who value relationship and emotion over the facts. An associate quit a large company when the sales staff excitedly took a product to market before it was ready. The engineers excitement for a finished product didn't match the sales people's excitement of the sales and commissions. Maybe some analysis and logic have a place.

Analysis isn't good for everything, though. I would hope that when holding a baby, you would avoid thoughts of "Am I doing it right?" and simply enjoy and sense the miracle of life. Kinesthetic and Haptic styles have their unique benefits and consequences as well.

The key to maximum enjoyment in all your relationships and maximum success in your communication efforts is found by creating balance. By learning to appreciate each style, and learning how to borrow its strengths, you can meet every occasion with an appropriate, effective response. Before we can attain balance, however, we need to look at where we might be unbalanced, and to see how that lack of balance causes misunderstanding and poor communication.

For all of us, results are paramount in our minds. Whether our goals are material — like a sale, a new car, a home or a child — or less tangible — like more happiness, more harmony or more simplicity — we are always simply accomplishing results. Sometimes that accomplishment requires new learning and understanding. Interestingly, once you learn and practice these tools in one area of your life, you can use the same skills quite effectively in other areas.

The skill you're about to learn to help you achieve your goals and solve all your chllenges is simply expanding skills of communication. eyeTalk™ looks at communication in a new way, from the other person's point of view and communication style rather than our own.

Many people have spent their lives aspiring to live by the Golden Rule — treating others as they themselves wished to be treated, communicating with others the way they themselves like to communicate. This code of behavior has been a motto for many wholesome, well-wishing people. The idea has been influential among people of very different cultures. Jesus, Hillel, and Confucius used it to summarize their caring teachings. From Jesus, "love one another as I have loved you" to the Buddhist "Hurt not others in ways that you would find hurtful," to the Islamic "No one of you is a believer until he desires for his brother that which he desires for himself," the idea that treating others with the same level of respect we wish to receive flavors all religious teaching.

Around the world and throughout time, this concept has been a common thread for caring, humane interactions and building of true community. And it was a good rule for centuries. As the world becomes increasingly a single interacting global community, however, we need to reconsider the wording of our Golden Rule. In fact, with the diversity of cultures we interact with every day, it is important to expand the Golden Rule to remember the wise words of George Bernard Shaw in 1903:

"Do not do unto others as you would that they should do unto you. Their tastes may not be the same."

We have not changed the intent of the original Golden Rule, just the words — to more accurately reflect the needs of others. A new Golden Rule, usually called the Platinum Rule still requires self-awareness and also awareness of others. The Platinum Rule by Dr. Tony Alessandra identifies the Director, Socializer, Relater, and Thinker What if the person I'm interacting with has different standards, cultural needs, and wishes? What if he or she has a different understanding of what constitutes polite or nurturing behavior?

The Platinum Rule takes away the old assumption that all other people would like to be treated the way that you would like to be treated. The original Golden Rule certainly no longer applies in communication. Let's say my only language is English and I'm in China, surrounded by people who speak only Chinese. If I treat others the way that I want to be treated, I will speak only English, and I will have little success in communication. Wouldn't it make more sense to treat the natives the way they want to be treated? Chinese people prefer speaking Chinese, and certainly appreciate an attempt at speaking their native tongue. As do all cultures.

We live in a global community; we all must learn to communicate more fullyl. The need for understanding is at an all-time high, and it begins with communication. Now is the time to expand our understanding of communication styles. With the infinite variety of ways to communicate, we must begin to understand our "best style" or preferred style of communication. Furthermore, we must learn the styles of others to consciously and efficiently communicate with those around us.

While I was traveling in Europe, one incident dramatically demonstrated communication preferences to me. I speak some German and regularly conversed with natives while in Germany. We spoke a combination of English and German, as their English was better than my German. They were gracious, and we had long, engaging conversations.

One evening, an American abruptly blurted out to my German friend, "Do you speak English?"

My friend felt that this interruption was impolite and answered, "Ich kann Sie nicht verstehen!" (I can't understand you.) Because that particular American chose not to try to speak his language, he would not speak English in reply, though he spoke our language impeccably. Even with his unwillingness to speak to the person, however, he used the respectful form of "you" rather than the more familiar "du."

When teaching English lessons in Holland, the instructors first say the Dutch word, then the English word, then the American pronunciation. Europeans know that to truly learn about another culture, it's important to learn their language and even their dialects. Europeans understand the Platinum Rule™: "Treat others the way they want to be treated" is especially important in communication. It respects and honors the feelings of others. Interacting with others shifts from "I want this, so I'll give everyone else the same thing," to "I'll find out what others want and then I'll give it to them." That creates rapport and appreciation.

Creating rapport is important in sales, management, personal relationships and everyday life. After all, no matter what the product or need, a salesperson would have little success selling in a language other than the client's. How many buyers would have a dim view of the salesperson who assumes their product is the only right one for the buyer, and approaches the sale without considering the buyer's needs? People do have different needs, wants, and ways of doing things. We should look at each buyer individually and serve their needs rather than forcing the one-size-fits-all approach. This idea is equally valuable between employers and employees, members of a team, teachers and students, parents and children, or husbands and wives.

How often have we heard something we simply wish to hear that is not really said at all? How many times have our feelings been hurt even with loving words? How often do we create separations with the wrong glance or the wrong tone at the most inauspicious time? This absence of complete alignment creates more discord in our relationships than you can imagine. For the most part, we accomplish disharmony so subtly, almost invisibly, simply because of an absence of understanding the other person.

Dr. Stephen Covey, author of "The Seven Habits of Highly Effective People," said that, of the seven habits, Americans have the most problems with #5: "Seek first to understand, then seek to be understood."

The author of the St. Francis prayer also understood this when he said, "Grant that I may seek not so much to be understood, as to understand."

How can we understand each other more? Believe it or not, greater understanding can begin with something as simple as looking into one another's eyes.

Imagine that someone you've never met before looks you in the eye and immediately gives you an accurate description of your personality, your talents and abilities, your preferred learning style, your communication style, and your relationships with friends and loved ones. And then, before you can recover from your astonishment, he offers to teach you the technique he used. Would you be intrigued?

After years of research and practice in communication, I've learned that each of us has a different learning/communication style and speaks a different, hidden language. These languages are called Visual, Auditory, Kinesthetic, and Haptic, and a person's language preference can actually be seen in their eyes. To help explain this phenomenon, I synthesized the eyeTalk. eyeTalk helps us see the four unique patterns contained in the iris of everyone's eyes. Each of these four patterns also has four different and distinct dialects of the language that is natural to them. Noticing eye patterns allows us to come to a deeper understanding and acceptance of others and ourselves.

In 1982, Denny Johnson wrote a revolutionary book, "What the Eye Reveals," in which he outlines a psychological profile based on patterns in the iris of the eye. This profile, known as the Rayid Model, has been proclaimed by researchers as 97% accurate. It lends credence to the age-old saying, "The eyes are the windows to the soul." eyeTalk™ combines the Rayid Model and Neuro-Linguistic Programming.

Dr. Hester Lewis, Harvard Medical School, School of Psychiatry, lauds the Rayid Model: "The future will prove Rayid a leader in counseling techniques. Using it along with what we know about human behavior, we can more wholly problem-solve and integrate questions on educational, career and marital choices and how to change personal, familial or parental attitudes and behavior."

Eye patterns indicate a hidden language. When you think of your eye pattern/learning/language style as a language, it's obvious that each different eye pattern could have a different language. Many people wonder whether eye patterns change when behaviors change, but the configurations in your eye formed before you were seven years old and will remain the same. Your "natural" language can be enhanced with others, but won't change.

With some close observations of the iris of the eye, you will understand your own hidden language and the hidden language of those around you. What do your eyes say? Let's look at some eyes closely.

What remarkable patterns! You may notice the patterns more clearly in the following diagram.

Amazingly, each pattern exposes some common behaviors. Spots or flecks indicate the Visual style of person, rounded openings indicate the Auditory style, straight lines indicate the Kinesthetic style, and combinations of all three patterns indicate the Haptic style.

The eyes are a visual aid for understanding these styles, and as we learn about these styles, we'll see patterns of behavior that exist in the body, the tone of voice, the way of living in the world. As with all patterns, they are only indicators of quality of life and relationship, and these patterns only determine behavior with an absence of awareness. With conscious awareness, any pattern may be changed.

All eyes are unique and often as opposite in appearance as in behavior. Let's look at some of these patterns more closely.

Visual. The Visual style develops a sensory acuity that allows for magnificent analysis and visualization. Visuals can program personal computers and flights to the moon, and develop solutions to the most complex human dilemmas of personal and societal health. While Visual people enjoy natural credibility, they often have difficulty establishing rapport in their relationships. All people with dot-like pigments in the iris of their eyes naturally communicate/ learn visually and demonstrate the characteristics summarized next to the eye above. We will learn to recognize Visual people, to understand their preferences, and to speak their hidden language.

Auditory, how to recognize Auditories even beyond their eye pattern, and how best to connect with this style. Auditory gifts include the ability to build relationships easily and refined skills of human interaction that can build family and refined skills of human interaction that can build family and team cohesion. The Auditory style appreciates emotions like love and peace, and calmly survives the desolation of grief and sadness. With its feeling state, this style allows for spontaneous expression and fosters vigorous change. These folks sow the seeds for growth and, with individual growth, our world grows.

THE VISUAL LANGUAGE STYLE

(Mental Type)

• Dot-like

• Processes through Eyes

• Fact-oriented

• Uses Analytical Thinking

• Often Opinionated

• Favorite Verbs: I see, I think

• Excels at Detail, Credibility, Clarity

THE AUDITORY LANGUAGE STYLE

(Feeling Type)

• Flower-petal openings

• Relationship Oriented

• Favorite Pronoun: "You"

• Favorite Verbs: I feel, I hear

• Excels at: Joy, Vision, Sociability, Rapport

The Kinesthetic style's strengths are sensitivity and subtlety. Kinesthetics are highly attuned to the importance of honor and respect, and know that the minutest of details is crucial for an impeccable life. Touch is very important to people with the Kinesthetic style. Because of their sensitivity, Kinesthetics often find the world harsh. The Kinesthetic eye pattern shows wispy, straight lines.

Haptic personality – the dynamics and excitement of a three-ring circus and a barrel of monkeys all rolled into one. The Haptic talents of speed, perspective, synthesis, and integration lead us to a vitality and joy not experienced by everyone. Sometimes Haptics appear scattered and frantic, but it's just their way: they combine the traits of all three of the other personalities, and process information using Visual, Auditory and Kinesthetic methods. Their eyes also demonstrate this combination of personalities, exhibiting traits of all the other three types. Haptic eyes are identified by the presence of all three patterns: dots, petal-like openings, and straight lines.

You may find it helpful to consider the languages of the eyeTalk™ as gears of a car. The first cars had a manual transmission and three gears. First gear is best for starting off. Second gear moves between first and second and is a transition gear. It relates to both first and third gear and moves between each of them. Third gear is the smoothest, but doesn't do well with starting and stopping. It's the freeway gear and is best when running at the higher speeds. Third gear allows only subtle changes and is the most efficient when running at high speeds.

The Visual language style is like first gear in a car. Through observation, Visual people plan and observe situations for the best outcome. They might not go fast, but they are great starting out. Staying in first gear all the time, our cars would operate less efficiently and wear out sooner. The same is true for Visual people.

THE KINESTHETIC LANGUAGE STYLE

(Physical Type)

• Straight lines/streaks, no dots or openings

• Senses with Whole Body

• Empathetic, Balanced

• Favorite Pronoun: "We"

• Uses verbs: I'm touched, I sense

• Excels at: Stillness, Connection, Mediation, Amiableness, Balance & Service

THE HAPTIC LANGUAGE STYLE

(Movement Type)

• Dots and Openings

• Dynamic Change, Transitioning

• Risk-Oriented, Driven, Zealous

• Motivated by Originality, Achievement

• Entrepreneurial

• Favorite Pronoun: "They"

• Uses verbs: Think, Feel and Act

• Moves Quickly

• Excels at Vitality, Joy, Activity, Achievement, Change

The Auditory language style is like second gear. It can be used for starting out, but only with difficulty. In second gear the car can go pretty fast, and it always keeps the motor going very fast. The second gear is noted for change. Once it gets going, second gear is flexible, allowing increases and decreases in speed. It is often noisier, and is the gear that requires the most shifting. Second gear is in relationship with lots of things. Everything that is around it affects it. It is in relationship with first gear, third gear, the motor, the clutch, traffic conditions, and the style of the driver.

Kinesthetic people could be considered third gear. The Kinesthetic runs best with smooth operation; subtle shifts in speed feel best to them. The same is true for third gear. To start off in a car with third gear is next to impossible. Likewise, because of their subtle nature, Kinesthetic people do much better at minor changes than at starting or stopping.

Haptic people could easily be described as the clutch, moving effortlessly from gear to gear, allowing all the styles to be used depending on the situation. The clutch is nothing without the gears, and the gears would operate less efficiently without a clutch.

All the eyes we've seen are different, with unique patterns of rounded openings, flecks, and lines. In the Rayid Model, Denny Johnson identified 46 characteristics that indicate a particular psychological profile!

This road map of the eyes has proven to be remarkably accurate. For more information about each of the 46 characteristics, consult Johnson's "What the Eye Reveals."

Here are some patterns of couples demonstrating that opposites really do attract each other.

The incredible work of art called our eyes reflects our individual magnificence. Each of us is unique, with an infinite combination of Visual, Auditory, Kinesthetic, Haptic, with an equally varied spectrum of volumes, shades, colors, and senses within our expression of who we are and how we live. Our natural eye pattern, automatically and quite inevitably, guide our preferences to become our choices. Our choices become habits. Soon our habits become our identity, and we only speak our hidden language. Without understanding our own language, and the language of those around us, we soon find ourselves disconnected from those around us.

Now is the time to know your best communication style, know the one's of those in your life and begin to build bridges of connection.

Everyone wants a simple answer, on how to communicate effectively, with one gender or another, one culture or another, one generation or another. We have just begun to explore:

How can a Visual style best can communicate with a Haptic one?

How do different generations change that answer?

How do cultures, genders, hierarchy also effect that answer?

And what about if someone is right brain or left brain?

Would a Right Brain Visual Internal Male, communicate the same or differently, as a Left Brain Visual External Female?

The answer begins with avoiding judgment and ends with extending appreciation.

It is time to appreciate each other. As Voltaire said, "Appreciation is a wonderful thing. It makes what is excellent in others belong to us as well." Appreciation begins with observation and continues with emulation. And certainly is dissipated by judgment and wrong making. Learning from another, and following their example, is the highest form of compliment. And ultimately becoming more than we were without new learning, and

Understanding and using eyeTalk and the other concepts in this book promises a balance between work and play, self and others, thinking and feeling sensitivity and excitement, reflection and expression, logic and intuition. Equally important, it lays the foundations for learning to communicate more fully and effectively with people who have preferences different from your own. Communication is both an art and a science. Using eyeTalk's powerful tools, you'll experience true artistry and discover real magic!

*"Seek first to understand,
then seek to be understood."*

- Dr. Stephen Covey

Summary

My goal with Herding Ostriches is to draw the attention of American businesses towards the art of generational leadership. This area of study will intensify over the next decade, and with six separate generational philosophies blending, this information will be central to hiring, growing and designing successful teams.

One thing that I am often asked to address is how to effectively managing fast growth and its growing pains in light of generational mixing. We have pure chaos if we don't factor it in. Before I advise anyone, I want to know the generational mix by numbers and positions within a company. It is the first thing that I want to consider before setting an action plan for growth. The generational mix will define how quickly we can move and in which direction are we most likely to be supported by the team. It takes a design board to map it out.

The economy has been like a wrench thrown into the middle of an already spinning wheel. At first, the economy forced painful downsizing, and now it is pushing more company mergers and acquisitions than ever seen in US history. We appear to be growing again, but in the most unexpected ways. Technology options and international influence are also tugging on the steering wheel.

I still see great leaders rising up to the challenge. They are what I refer to as the "smooth ducks" of business. They appear to be gliding along effortlessly on a still lake. I know that underneath that smooth surface, they have to be doing some powerful paddling. They are working through the generational leadership. I see them mastering emotional intelligence and adapting their communication to the receiver. I see them leading with the iron fist in the velvet glove. I see teams that are operating smoothly while realize the opportunity for individual growth. I see teams that don't even seem to realize that they are being managed. They operate with a sense of individual purpose.

These leaders are herding ostriches and not running in circles or sticking their heads in the sand. They are using all five principles laid out in this book. They are looking forward and preparing for the next phase. They still look like smooth ducks to me. I even hear them humming as they leave work for the day.

I don't know why it works, it just does.

About Contributor
Kevin Brooks

Kevin Brooks resides in Nashville, Tennessee and has made his entire career about distance sales and service. He specializes in personalized sales and service, telephone techniques, call centers, and developing scripts that can connect people when the spoken word is all they have.

He learned most of his technique by traveling with his father as a young boy in Atlanta. He spent his summers watching first hand as his dad, an award-winning corporate sales director, mastered the art of connection.

"People think that you are a good salesperson if you have the gift of gab. Nothing could be further from the truth. You need the gift of listening. They will only care about your product or service if they first believe that you care about them."

Email: brucekbrooks@comcast.net

About Contributor
Seth Johnson

S eth Johnson graduated with a B.S. in Mathematics from the University of Stony Brook. He has a Master's in Education from Boston College.

He resides in Boston.

Seth specializes in social and emotional development. He is on a mission to cure poverty. He hopes that you will join him.

Email: goldenhemloc11@hotmail.com

ABOUT CONTRIBUTOR JOHN MELUSO

John Meluso is an internationally acclaimed speaker and is the author of three books:

Eyetalk TM – Bridging from Communications to Connection

The Divine Secret: The Legend of Og

The Next Step for Positive Living, co-authored with Joseph Bernard, PhD

Email: johncsp@meluso.com

About the Author
Kate Sheridan

Kate Sheridan is a professional speaker, and the CEO of 15 Minute Books. She is also the co-founder and original CEO of Help a Child Smile Mobile Medicine.

Sheridan is a former journalist and has directed award-winning teams of up to 750. She resides in Nashville and Atlanta.

Email: katesheridan27@gmail.com

Get your head out of the sand!